SUBJECTIVITY

Ideal for anyone who has ever asked 'Who am I?', *Subjectivity* explores the history of theories of selfhood, from the Classical era to the present, and demonstrates how those theories can be applied in literary and cultural criticism.

Donald E. Hall:

- examines all of the major methodologies and theoretical emphases of the twentieth and twenty-first centuries, including psychoanalytic criticism, materialism, feminism, and queer theory
- applies the theories discussed in detailed readings of literary and cultural texts, from novels and poetry to film and the visual arts
- offers a unique perspective on our current obsession with perfecting our selves
- looks to the future of selfhood in a time of new technologies and identity possibilities.

Examining some of the most exciting issues confronting cultural critics and readers today, *Subjectivity* is the essential introduction to a fraught but crucial critical term and a challenge to the way we define our selves.

Donald E. Hall is Chair of the Department of English at California State University, Northridge. His previous publications include *Literary and Cultural Theory: From Basic Principles to Advanced Applications* (2001) and *Queer Theories* (2003).

THE NEW CRITICAL IDIOM

SERIES EDITOR: JOHN DRAKAKIS, UNIVERSITY OF STIRLING

The New Critical Idiom is an invaluable series of introductory guides to today's critical terminology. Each book:

- provides a handy, explanatory guide to the use (and abuse) of the term
- offers an original and distinctive overview by a leading literary and cultural critic
- relates the term to the larger field of cultural representation.

With a strong emphasis on clarity, lively debate, and the widest possible breadth of examples, *The New Critical Idiom* is an indispensable approach to key topics in literary studies.

Also available in this series:

Autobiography by Linda Anderson

Class by Gary Day

Colonialism/Postcolonialism by Ania Loomba

Culture/Metaculture by Francis Mulhern

Discourse by Sara Mills

Dramatic Monologue by Glennis Byron

Genders by David Glover and Cora Kaplan

Gothic by Fred Botting

Historicism by Paul Hamilton

Humanism by Tony Davies

Ideology by David Hawkes

Interdisciplinarity by Joe Moran

Intertextuality by Graham Allen

Irony by Claire Colebrook

Literature by Peter Widdowson

Metre, Rhythm and Verse Form by Philip Hobsbaum

Modernism by Peter Childs

Myth by Laurence Coupe

Narrative by Paul Cobley

Parody by Simon Dentith

Pastoral by Terry Gifford

Realism by Pam Morris

Romanticism by Aidan Day

Science Fiction by Adam Roberts

Sexuality by Joseph Bristow

Stylistics by Richard Bradford

The Unconscious by Antony Easthope

SUBJECTIVITY

Donald E. Hall

Routledge
Taylor & Francis Group

NEW YORK AND LONDON

First published 2004
by Routledge
270 Madison Avenue, New York, NY 10016

Simultaneously published in the UK
by Routledge
2 Park Square, Milton Park, Abingdon, Oxon OX14 4RN

Transferred to Digital Printing 2006

Routledge is an imprint of the Taylor & Francis Group, an informa business

© 2004 Donald E. Hall

Typeset in Adobe Garamond and Scala Sans by
Keystroke, Jacaranda Lodge, Wolverhampton
Printed and bound in Great Britain by
Biddles Ltd, King's Lynn, Norfolk

Library of Congress Cataloging in Publication Data
Hall, Donald E. (Donald Eugene), 1960–
    Subjectivity/Donald E. Hall.
      p. cm. – (The new critical idiom)
    Includes bibliographical references and index.
    1. Self-knowledge in literature. 2. Subjectivity in literature.
    3. Literature, Modern–History and criticism. I. Title. II. Series.
    PN56.S46H35 2004
    809'.93353–dc22   2003017131

British Library Cataloguing in Publication Data
A catalogue record for this book is available from the British Library

ISBN 13: 978-0-415-28762-3 (pbk)
ISBN 10: 0-415-28762-6 (pbk)

Contents

Series Editor's Preface   vii

Introduction   1
What is Subjectivity?   1
Classical and Pre-modern Identities   6

1 The Early Modern Era and Enlightenment   16
Descartes and the "I"   16
Locke, Kant, and the "We"   23

2 The Nineteenth and Early Twentieth Centuries   32
Slavery and Subjectivities   32
Wollstonecraft and Early Feminist Subjectivity   39
Marx, Hegel, and Class Subjectivity   49
Freud and the Rise of the Social Sciences   57
Nietzsche and the Existentialists   67

3 The Politics of Identity   78
Lacan   78
Althusser   84
Foucault and Discourse Theory   90
The Politics of Gender and Sexuality   97
Race and Postcoloniality   110

4 Postmodernism and the Question of Agency   118
Haraway and Cyborg Subjectivity   118
Subjectivities   124

Glossary   131
Bibliography   135
Index   142

SERIES EDITOR'S PREFACE

The New Critical Idiom is a series of introductory books which seeks to extend the lexicon of literary terms, in order to address the radical changes which have taken place in the study of literature during the last decades of the twentieth century. The aim is to provide clear, well-illustrated accounts of the full range of terminology currently in use, and to evolve histories of its changing usage.

The current state of the discipline of literary studies is one where there is considerable debate concerning basic questions of terminology. This involves, among other things, the boundaries which distinguish the literary from the non-literary; the position of literature within the larger sphere of culture; the relationship between literatures of different cultures; and questions concerning the relation of literary to other cultural forms within the context of interdisciplinary studies.

It is clear that the field of literary criticism and theory is a dynamic and heterogeneous one. The present need is for individual volumes on terms which combine clarity of exposition with an adventurousness of perspective and a breadth of application. Each volume will contain as part of its apparatus some indication of the direction in which the definition of particular terms is likely to move, as well as expanding the disciplinary boundaries within which some of these terms have been traditionally contained. This will involve some re-situation of terms within the larger field of cultural representation, and will introduce examples from the area of film and the modern media in addition to examples from a variety of literary texts.

INTRODUCTION

WHAT IS SUBJECTIVITY?

"Who am I?" is a question that has been pondered, no doubt, by all of us at some point, perhaps at many and various points, in our lives. Indeed, we live in an era in which we are commonly asked to rethink, express, and explain our identities by a wide variety of authority figures and institutions: parents, school guidance counselors, best-selling self-help gurus, talk show hosts, and even advertisers, who encourage us to test out a different form of "self" expression by purchasing an expensive car, entering a weight-loss program, or trying a new hair color. We are widely led to believe that we have the freedom and ability to create and re-create our "selves" at will, if we *have* the will, but at the same time are presented with a suspiciously narrow range of options and avenues that will allow us to fit comfortably into society and our particular gendered, regional, ethnic, sexual subset of it.

Legal theorist and social historian Lawrence M. Friedman interprets this as the result of a gradual move from a "vertical" (hierarchical, inflexible) to a more "horizontal" (negotiable, agency-driven) mode of defining our relationships to each other, one in which we are laden with the responsibility for "making something" of ourselves. He argues in *The Horizontal Society* that we live in an age "in which old forms and traditions seem to be breaking down – forms and traditions that trapped the individual in a cage of ascription; that fixed human beings in definite social roles, pinned them to a given position in the world, no matter how they might wriggle and fight" (Friedman 1999: vii–viii). At the end of his investigation of both possibilities for and limitations imposed upon "self" creation in contemporary society, he concludes that today "one even chooses (within limits) a race, a gender, a form of sexuality. One can also choose *not* to be counted as part of any particular group, though this is sometimes more difficult, because the outside society does not always go along with one's choices" (240). He further complicates the matter in stating that

> choice is often an illusion. People are firm believers in free will. But they choose their politics, their dress, their manners, their very identity, from a menu they had no hand in writing. They are constrained by forces they do not understand and are not even conscious of. But even the *illusion* of choice is of enormous social significance.
>
> (240)

The many issues he raises, such as those of freedom and constraint, and of self-construction and social construction, are not only some of the most highly contested in current critical and sociological theory, but also in the entire history of philosophy, psychology, and theology. Friedman's commentary and qualifications direct us, in fact, to the very subject matter of *Subjectivity*: that tension between choice and illusion, between imposed definitions and individual interrogations of them, and between old formulae and new responsibilities, especially as those tensions help us to understand the intersection of literary and other forms of cultural representation, and the critical/theoretical discussion of identity and identity politics.

The term "subjectivity," as Regenia Gagnier has argued in her incisive investigation of Victorian self-representation, can mean in critical parlance today many things simultaneously:

> First, the subject is a subject to itself, an "I," however difficult or even impossible it may be for others to understand this "I" from its own viewpoint, within its own experience. Simultaneously, the subject is a

subject to, and of, others; in fact, it is often an "Other" to others, which also affects its sense of its own subjectivity. . . . Third, the subject is also a subject of knowledge, most familiarly perhaps of the discourse of social institutions that circumscribe its terms of being. Fourth, the subject is a body that is separate (except in the case of pregnant women) from other human bodies; and the body, and therefore the subject, is closely dependent upon its physical environment.

(Gagnier 1991: 8)

But all of these delineations of the "subject," she concludes, are also bound up with the simple distinction commonly attributed to the seventeenth-century philosopher René Descartes of the difference between "objectivity," the perspective of impartial "truth," and "subjectivity," the limited, error-prone perspective of the individual (9). While Descartes, to whom we will return in later chapters, never actually uses the terms "subjective" or "subjectivity," he ends his sixth "Meditation" with the humble admission that "the life of man is very often subject to error" (Descartes 1968: 169), because one's perspective is always partial, imperfect, or, in other words, human. And these limitations include, of course, our ability to know in any full or reliable way our "selves."

Yet as we will explore in Chapter 1, these unavoidable limitations certainly did not keep Descartes from struggling to think about the "self." Indeed, his famous delineation in his *Discourse on Method* of the *cogito* – "I think, therefore I am" – sets out his definition of human "being" itself as one of struggling to know in spite of the futility of ever knowing completely. And this is why the term "subjectivity" is such a useful one, meaning as it does something slightly different from the term identity, although the two terms have sometimes been used interchangeably. For our purposes, one's identity can be thought of as that particular set of traits, beliefs, and allegiances that, in short- or long-term ways, gives one a consistent personality and mode of social being, while subjectivity implies always a degree of thought and self-consciousness about identity, at the same time allowing a myriad of limitations and often unknowable, unavoidable constraints on our ability to fully comprehend identity. Subjectivity as a critical concept invites us to consider the question of how and from where identity arises, to what extent it is understandable, and to what degree it is something over which we have any measure of influence or control. In the concise delineation of Ross Murfin and Supryia Ray, the authors of *The Bedford Glossary of Critical and Literary Terms*, subjectivity points "to that which we would (but may be unable to) know, that which we do (or believe ourselves to) know, and individual or cultural ways of knowing – or of trying to know" (Murfin and Ray 1997: 388). In this way, subjectivity is the intersection of two lines of philosophical inquiry: epistemology (the study of how we know what we know) and ontology (the study of the nature of being or existence). In other words, inquiries into subjectivity might ask, "How does our understanding of knowledge relate to, impact, and/or constrain our understanding of our own existence?" Indeed, one question that follows is: "Is our social and individual existence determined by the ways that we collectively organize knowledge?"

But before we begin to explore the various ways in which these questions have been posed, answered, or wholly ignored over the course of many centuries, it is worth pondering for a moment why this is pertinent to or imagined to be within the broad domain of literary and cultural criticism. For much of human history, these were religious, philosophical, and political questions, but hardly constituted the driving impulse behind critical examinations of novels, poetry, plays, and other forms of aesthetic representation. Literary and cultural theory today asks what the feminist theorist Elaine Marks calls the "'big questions,' the big metaphysical ones that [have] dropped out of Anglo-American philosophy: life and death and the meaning of love" (Marks 2001: 277). Joe Moran notes that these "big questions" include those addressing "the nature of reality, language, power, gender, sexuality, the body, and the self" (Moran 2002: 83). Of course, these are questions that religion once asked and firmly answered, but whose responses, especially in the post-Darwinian era, are no longer satisfying or even credible. Moreover, as Anglo-American philosophy in the twentieth century gravitated toward more analytical and quantifiable methodologies, these "big questions" became the domain of Continental philosophers (French and German in particular) and the Anglo-American literary critics who read and used them.

That is not, however, the only reason why subjectivity is of interest to students of literature and culture, especially given the fact that traditional literary studies have broadened now to include a diverse array of texts beyond those of poems, novels, and plays. We come to texts today looking not only for forms of entertainment and instruction, but also for reasons that are politically driven and connected to agendas well beyond aesthetic understanding. Identity became thoroughly politicized in the nineteenth and twentieth centuries and part of our continuing struggle to understand the different ways in which identities are socially valued, interrogated, and replicated is through the process of reading, studying, and critically engaging with a wide variety of cultural texts. Indeed, as literary and cultural critics have aggressively expanded what they mean by the term text, the textuality of the self as a system of representations has, itself, become a singularly important arena of investigation and speculation. Thus in exploring subjectivity, we are in effect exploring the "self" as a text, as a topic for critical analysis, both in and beyond its relationship to the traditional texts of literature and culture.

In the following chapters we will traverse many centuries of inquiry and a wide array of current literary/cultural critical methodologies. Every major critical movement of the mid- to late twentieth century touched, in some form or fashion, on notions of subjectivity, even as they often suggested very different answers to the same questions concerning "who" and "what" we are, "how" we became and "why" we remain that which we are, and to what extent we have both the capacity and the ability to become something different. Thus the issue with which this book will grapple, as it looks not just at the distant and near past, but also the present and future, is that of "agency," a controversial topic that has been at the center of discussions of subjectivity for centuries, and one that will never be wholly put to rest, even as it remains compelling. For in probing agency, we are, in effect, tackling the fundamental question of responsibility: in personal action, in aesthetic creation, in inter-personal norms and social valuations. For theoreticians of subjectivity, especially those of late, a central concern is how we should – and to what extent we even have an ability to – change society through concerted individual action, and the ways that cultural representation can, does, or does not abet those changes. These are questions that were not always asked in earlier eras of human history, but that once asked, could never be wholly withdrawn or forgotten. As we shall see, for all of these reasons and many more, the topic of "subjectivity" is one of unparalleled and enduring importance.

CLASSICAL AND PRE-MODERN IDENTITIES

I stated earlier that certain questions regarding responsibility and agency in the creation and maintenance of the "self" are ones that were not always asked if we look back through many centuries of time. To be sure, human beings, for as long as we have written records of our thoughts and creative output, have always pondered the question "who am I?" However, the degree to which the pondering "I" is perceived as having any specific role in, or responsibility for, creating its own "selfhood" has changed dramatically over time. In fact, that is one common way that historians and critics differentiate the pre-modern and modern eras, as those terms signal dramatic shifts in social structures and social meaning-making when the Middle Ages gave way to the Renaissance. Stephen Greenblatt argues in his influential work *Renaissance Self-Fashioning: From More to Shakespeare* that

> there is in the early modern period a change in the intellectual, social, psychological, and aesthetic structures that govern the generation of identities. . . . Perhaps the simplest observation that we can make is that in the sixteenth century there appears to be an increased self-consciousness about the fashioning of human identity as a manipulable, artful process.
>
> (Greenblatt 1980: 1–2)

Greenblatt argues that we can find a few precursors to this "self-consciousness . . . among the elite in the classical world, but [then] Christianity brought a growing suspicion of man's power to shape identity" (2). Yet even during the classical era we find no real equivalent of the emphasis on self-creation that arises during the Renaissance and that expands dramatically during later centuries.

Indeed, the stark limitations on who had the right or ability to participate in even highly limited forms of self-fashioning in classical thinking certainly makes the classical worldview much closer to that of the medieval era than that of the modern era. This continuity between classical and medieval thinking is one of Charles Taylor's main points in his important study *Sources of the Self: The Making of the Modern Identity*. He notes that the "modern aspiration for meaning and substance in one's life has obvious affinities with longer-standing aspirations to higher being, to immortality" (Taylor 1989: 43). Yet he differentiates clearly between pre-modern and modern ways in which that meaning and substance is theorized. In pre-modern eras, philosophers and writers often "invoke some larger reality we should connect with," as, for example, in the thirteenth century, when

> St. Francis left his companions and family and the life of a rich and popular young man in Assisi, he must have felt in his own terms, the insubstantiality of that life and have been looking for something fuller, wholer, to give himself more integrally to God, without stint.
>
> (43)

Yet this search outward for a defining connection not only characterized the early Christian era, but the classical era as well, though certainly for Greek philosophers, the looking outward for "meaning and substance" was framed in historically specific ways.

Plato (c. 429–347 BC) provides a useful case in point. In Taylor's assessment, Plato's "rule of reason is to be understood as rule by a rational vision of order. . . . To be ruled by reason means to have one's life shaped by a pre-existent rational order which one knows and loves" (124). And this clearly makes Plato's perspective on identity and agency very different from the ones that we will explore later, for as Taylor notes, modern identity arises in the "replacement of this understanding of the dominance of reason by another, more readily accessible to our minds, in which the order involved in the paramountcy of reason is *made*, not found" (124). In ways that may seem quite foreign to us, the notion of society working ideally through the discovery of, and adherence to, *preordained* truths and patterns resonates throughout classical thought. As T. Z. Lavine has noted, for Plato and his contemporaries "every state of whatever type necessarily has three parts which are its three social classes – a producer class, a military class, and a governing or ruling class" (Lavine 1984: 57–58). He continues, "In the ideal city, the Republic which Socrates and his young disciples are designing, each of these three classes will perform a vital function on behalf of the organic totality which is the society" (58). Under no circumstances, of course, is self-determination a part of what they considered healthy or rational. Thus in book 4 of Plato's *Republic*, Socrates, under intense questioning, states bluntly, "we are fashioning the happy State, not piecemeal, or with a view of making a few happy citizens, but as a whole," for if happiness is approached individualistically the State may well turn "upside down": "the husbandman will be no longer a husbandman, the potter will cease to be a potter, and no one will have the character of any distinct class" (Plato 1973: 109). Taylor notes that even for Plato's best-known critic, Aristotle, "wisdom is a kind of awareness of order, the correct order of ends in my life, which integrates all of my goals into a unified whole in which each has its proper weight" (Taylor 1989: 125). Yet the success of this inward correctness is dependent wholly on one's knowledge of larger patterns:

> The good life for human beings is as it is because of humans' nature as rational life. Humanity is part of the order of beings, each with its own nature. Each kind of thing . . . strives to reach its perfection and hence fulfills its nature. As agents, striving for ethical excellence, humans thus participate in the same rational order which they can also contemplate and admire in science.
>
> (125)

In this worldview, we only act ethically when we act in fulfillment of our preordained purpose, in concert with our duty to our society and its subunits.

This theme is pervasive in the literature of the era and is, of course, memorably portrayed in Sophocles' tragedy *Antigone* (*c.*441 BC). The question posed by the play is not *what* our duty or purpose is, or *how* to discover it, but simply whether or not we will fulfill divine decrees that are clear and incontrovertible. When the play's heroine Antigone learns that the ruler Creon has ordered that the corpse of her rebellious brother will remain "unwept, unsepulchered, a welcome object for the birds, when they spy him, to feast on at will" (Sophocles 1967: 118), she puts the simple question to her sister Ismene of "whether you are nobly bred or the base daughter of a noble line" (118). Of course, both sisters know well their obligation to their brother, that they are required by duty to bury him in spite of Creon's unethical decree. When Ismene demurs – "to defy the state – I have no strength for that. . . . How I fear for you!"

– Antigone retorts, almost mechanically, "Do not fear for me; guide your own fate aright" (119). After she is caught by guards and questioned by Creon about her disobedience of his orders, Antigone remains steadfast in her ethical understanding: "it was not Zeus that had published that edict. . . . Nor did I deem that your decrees were of such force that a mortal could override the unwritten and unfailing statutes of heaven" (127). While part of the tension of the drama arises from the fact that Creon is acting within his own sense of a specifically human (social) ethics that makes him resist honoring the corpse of a rebel, the damning quality of his willfulness is made clear by the seer Teiresias:

> All men are liable to err; but when the error has been made, the man is no longer witless or unblest who heals the ill into which he has fallen and does not remain stubborn. . . . Self-will, we know, incurs the charge of folly. Nay, allow the claim of the dead; do not stab the fallen.
>
> (140)

Though Creon does finally relent, his admission of error comes too late, for his son commits suicide after the death of his betrothed Antigone, and his wife then kills herself too. The tragedy that is dramatized is brought about by Creon's indulgence in self-will, which in this context indicates an attempt to create a personal code of ethics rather than be guided by a predetermined and inflexible code of duty. Individuality is the problem; conformity and acquiescence to divine law are the solution.

Certainly the parameters within which thinkers continued to probe the tension between individuality and conformity changed during the first centuries of the Christian era, but the solutions validated in most religious and literary writings remain similar up to the Renaissance. In the book of Genesis, Adam and Eve are expelled from Eden because of their quest for knowledge, for their self-will in defiance of divine law. Only in living lives of obedience and faith will men and women ever be redeemed. As Taylor notes, the continuities between the worldviews of Plato and the fourth/fifth-century theologian St. Augustine are therefore quite striking:

> Augustine gives us a Platonic understanding of the universe as an external realization of a rational order. . . . God's eternal law enjoins

order. It calls on humans to see and respect this order. For Augustine as for Plato, the vision of cosmic order is the vision of reason, and for both the good of humans involves their seeing and loving this order.

(Taylor 1989: 128)

Indeed, Augustine in his *Confessions* extols the joys of submission: "O Lord . . . Thy whole gift was, to nill what I willed, and to will what Thou willedst. But where through all those years, and out of what low and deep recesses was my free-will called forth in a moment, whereby to submit my neck to Thy easy yoke, and my shoulders unto Thy light burden . . . ? How sweet did it at once become to me . . . !" (Augustine 1909: 144). Of course, there is no room in Augustinian thought for self-construction or agency in changing the self, except to bring one's actions into line with a larger truth. This involves thinking and introspection, to be sure, but with an express purpose:

my experience of my own thinking puts me in contact with a perfection. . . . [T]he perfection in question was that of eternal, unchanging truth, which operates as a common standard for our thought. This is both something essentially presupposed in our thinking and yet manifestly not our own product, argues Augustine.

(Taylor 1989: 140)

And while dramatic changes in the types of questions and answers offered in philosophy and literature were about to occur, and even were beginning to be raised sporadically, the literature of the medieval era continues to validate a form of static, healthy, and secure order through one's understanding of and adhering to a preordained place and a divine plan.

As Gary Day notes in his historical overview of changing conceptions of social class,

society of the Middle Ages . . . was divided into three estates: the clergy, whose business was with prayer and spiritual well-being; the warriors, who defended the land and the people with their arms; and the laborers who supported the other two. . . . It was believed that these divisions were divinely ordained and that birth determined destiny.

(Day 2001: 19)

He points to William Langland's *Piers the Ploughman* (1379) as an exemplary text of the era, when Langland writes that God "gave to some men Intelligence . . . by which to earn their living as preachers and priests. . . . He taught some men to ride out on horseback and recover unlawful gains by speed and strength of arm, and some he taught to till the soil, to ditch and to thatch" (cit. Day 2001: 20). That was the theory, at any rate. But the certainty with which Langland expresses this worldview belies the slowly, but inexorably changing nature of social structures and social understanding during the era. Day notes that a number of historical changes abetted what we might call the rise of "individuality" during the late medieval era, including the plague or "Black Death" of 1348–49, which helped make laborers newly aware of their own scarcity and value, and the "growth of commodity production, [which] together with the increase in the use of money, began to undermine the system of personal obligations that characterized feudalism" (22). The dominant social model remained that of a "status-based conception of the social order [which] assumes that stability not change is the governing principle of society. However, the late medieval world . . . was characterized by a number of developments that prefaced profound upheaval" (22).

One of the most widely recognized of these developments was the Peasants' Revolt of 1381, in which disgruntled laborers marched into London, burned houses, and killed the archbishop of Canterbury. As Robert M. Adams notes,

> in the background lay an ancient, deep-seated rancor against the heavy weight of the feudal overlords and the enormously wealthy, vastly overprivileged church. . . . In the common course of life they could not, dared not, rebel; but the Black Death and the depopulation it caused made [the peasants] aware of their importance to society, at the very moment when society through the harsh Statute of Laborers was bearing down on them more heavily than ever.
>
> (Adams 1983: 68–69)

Yet as Jeremy Black has argued, the goal of the self-interested rioters was not to overthrow the government or social system, or even to claim their "rights" in some modern sense. It was simply to pressure the government to change a few discrete policies, mostly concerning taxes (Black

1996: 65–66). And certainly their gains were meager and short-lived, since the leaders of the riots were killed and the status quo quickly reasserted.

Thus while the Peasants' Revolt indicated that the nature of identity was beginning to change, and that self-interest in clear defiance of supposedly "divine" mandate was thinkable and actionable by groups working collectively, certainly the literary castigation of such deviant thinking was not far afield from that evinced almost two millennia earlier in the plays of Sophocles. In *The Voice of One Crying*, written at the time of the uprising, the poet John Gower condemns self-assertion on the part of any of the three estates or social classes, but he reserves special scorn for the peasantry, for "God and Nature have ordained that they shall serve" (Gower 1962: 209). However, he does admit, tellingly, that in his own day "neither [God nor Nature] knows how to keep them within bounds" (209). And this does represent a noteworthy change from earlier time periods. Whereas for Sophocles, the punishment of Creon was swift and sure, for Gower, manifestations of self-will are far less quickly dispatched. He writes, "The serfs perform none of their servile duties voluntarily and have no respect for the law. Whatever the serf's body suffers patiently under compulsion, inwardly his mind turns toward utter wickedness" (209). However oppressive their situation may be, peasants have no right to protest: "It is not for man's estate that anyone from the class of serfs should try to set things right" (209). As in the classical era, an inward turn is seen as threatening the stability of the divine order and the smooth functioning of the estates model of medieval society. But this is no longer Creon's idiosyncratic deviation from divine mandate; this is group action arising from a form of self-awareness and group politicization. While we are still many centuries away from the rise in literacy that would allow members of the laboring classes to record their own thoughts and desires, even Gower's detached view of something like peasant subjectivity is intriguing, for servility in the quotation above is dependent upon a very fragile, voluntary adherence to the law and the ferocity of Gower's argument throughout *The Voice of One Crying* reveals just how potent the threat he perceived really was.

Given these limitations, how does the concept of subjectivity pertain to pre-modern identities? Certainly we must attend to nuances of difference. In exploring pre-modern belief systems, no one would suggest that individuality was unknown before the Renaissance. The finely drawn cast of characters in Chaucer's late fourteenth-century *Canterbury Tales* demonstrates the many idiosyncrasies and individual impulses underlying human behavior and identity. Indeed, the fact that individuals negotiated their own rules within and regarding the institution of marriage, as heavily regulated, narrowly and statically defined a structure as one could ever imagine, is quite clear in the diversity of expressions on that institution among Chaucer's *Knight's*, *Franklin's*, *Merchant's* and (most famously) *Wife of Bath's* tales and prologues. Of course, people had unique traits, and they chose each other as friends and lovers, distinguished themselves in battle and as benevolent rulers or despots, and even were elected Pope because of their differences and distinct abilities. Furthermore, and as we see above, inward mental activity or an active interior life was long seen as a possibility, even if a disturbing one, in its threat to social cohesion. Yet while we can see therein the very beginnings of modern subjectivity, at the same time, our current notion of self-consciousness, of being self-made or self-actualized, of assuming a *responsibility* for creating oneself out of the raw materials and opportunities provided, and of interrogating and rejecting some roles while trying on and individualizing others, was quite foreign, even if dramatic changes were in the wind.

Indeed, our own sympathy for the gradual, often difficult and harshly punished, struggle toward a modern notion of identity is one reason why the figure of Joan of Arc (*c.*1412–31) continues to intrigue us, continues to be the subject of drama, film, and biography. She existed on that cusp of modernity. In Joan, we find a young peasant girl of the late Middle Ages who follows her own path, deviates wholly from the norms of her day, dons men's clothing, enters battle, challenges her king, and then dies for her transgressions. Of course the viability of her individualism, the tenacity of her self-made quality, was wholly dependent upon her claims to (and probably steadfast personal belief in) having received a divine mandate. And however we may wish to interpret her today, as proto-feminist, as religious fanatic, or as savvy manipulator, she certainly did not survive long as a thoroughgoing social deviant. We cannot know how to characterize accurately Joan's subjectivity, or anything about her degree of self-knowledge or awareness of agency in a self-conscious construction and manipulation of identity, but we do know that she was quickly denounced and burned at the stake as a heretic. The implications of her acting out a form of even proto-subjectivity threatened the stability of class and gender definitions, even of the church and state. Today we love her because she seems so modern, brave, and individualistic; the Inquisition, of course, reviled her and other nonconformists because they represented a manifestation of aberrant agency outside of tradition and the strict defining power of conservative institutions and divine law.

In fact, that right to even a small degree of agency in subjectively knowing and incorporating biblical truth was the very cause of the Protestant reformation and of centuries of argument and warfare that continue to this day. Subjectivity, at least in implication, was at the center of Martin Luther's argument in his treatise "Concerning Christian Liberty" (1520) when he writes, "A Christian man is the most free lord of all, and subject to none; a Christian man is the most dutiful servant of all, and subject to every one" (Luther 1910: 363). While for Luther, being a "true Christian; that is a spiritual, new, and inward man" (363) was always a matter of steadfastly living God's will, that external reference was also always subject to considerable internal contemplation. Famously, this led to an extraordinary amount of anxiety in Luther over human freedom, since in breaking with Catholic church hierarchy, he was opening the door to individual interpretation of biblical texts and agency in the creation of religious truth. In this way, we might see subjectivity as bound inextricably to textual interpretation. Biblical truth and the truth of the self were both opened up to questioning and reinvention.

In the pre-modern era, both required limiting forces as well. To this day, literalism in biblical interpretation has always been a powerful force in Protestantism; the less authority granted to church hierarchy in interpretation, the more rigidly the individual is expected to hold to the fundamental truth of scripture. In *On the Bondage of the Will* (1525), Luther further qualified any self-expressive freedom in his articulation of a zealous belief in predetermination and steadfast assertion of the need to humble oneself totally before God, losing self-confidence in order to find a form of self-knowledge in self-abasement. In Ernst Cassirer's words in *The Philosophy of the Enlightenment*, "the religious individualism of the Reformation remains throughout oriented and confined to purely objective, supernaturally binding realities" (Cassirer

1951: 139). But as quasi-objectively based as Luther's attempt to limit the implications of his own rebellious individualism were, in fact, subjectivity remained at its core. And this is where my reading of Luther differs from that of Charles Taylor, who says that Luther's "intense anguish and distress before his liberating moment of insight about salvation through faith" was not "a crisis of meaning. This term would have made no sense to Luther in its modern use. . . . The 'meaning' of life was all too unquestionable for this Augustinian monk, as it was for his whole age" (Taylor 1989: 18). Whether or not Luther would have recognized a particular term is irrelevant, for his continuing anguish over, and revolutionary new theorizations of, Christian subjectivity reveal in fact an enormous crisis of social meaning in the late Middle Ages/early modern era over even a very small degree of individual agency in the interpretation and creation of selfhood.

Indeed, and as we will explore throughout the remainder of this book, that very small degree of agency, attended often by acute anguish and profound distress, is subjectivity as we continue to experience and live it today.

1

THE EARLY MODERN ERA
AND ENLIGHTENMENT

DESCARTES AND THE "I"

While the insights of what we term the "New Historicism" have thoroughly undermined the credibility of a neat and linear historical trajectory of progress and expansion of understanding (see Paul Hamilton's *Historicism* [1996] for a full discussion), it is still important to recognize that change does occur over time, and that there have been dramatic shifts in socio-political context and consciousness that justify our self-aware use of historical periodization, as an attempt to understand our past, present, and possible futures. Of course, historical categories such as "Medieval" and "Renaissance" are always reductive and can be used over-rigidly; they are backwards projections that cannot fully capture the ways that shifts in social organization and belief systems are gradual, halting, and experienced differently among classes, genders, and regions. Even so, it is quite clear that dramatically different ways of understanding the self and its relationship to the world were articulated and realized around AD 1500. Our explanations of this phenomenon will always be partial and tendentious, but exploring these shifts can still prove very useful as we lay the groundwork for eventually thinking about where we are today and where we would like to go in the new millennium that we have entered.

So much was happening in Western Europe and the British Isles around the fifteenth and sixteenth centuries that we might say that the emergence of "the modern identity," as Taylor refers to it, was over-determined during this historical period. Critics and theorists use the term "overdetermination" when so many separate, as well as overlapping, forces and factors account for a single occurrence or manifestation that no one cause can be isolated as a simple explanation. Indeed, the many social changes occurring around the time of the Renaissance are far too numerous to list here. The Christian Church splintered into Catholicism and Protestantism, and that was soon followed by the self-interested bickering of a wide variety of factions within the latter movement. The invention of the printing press and moveable type in the fifteenth century abetted a steady increase in literacy rates and an ever-widening circula-tion of new ideas and different perspectives on the world. Copernicus and then Galileo helped inaugurate a scientific revolution that pointed out man's lack of centrality in the universe, and demonstrated that science, rather than religion, could explain the world we see around us and also offer dramatic new means by which we might change that world. Indeed, by simply looking through Galileo's telescope the reality of perception was undermined significantly even as such technology suggested that man now had new forms of power over the natural world. Urbanization, because of population growth and a myriad of changes in rural social organization, brought increasing numbers of people into contact with each other, and face to face with an ever more diverse array of lives and outlooks. Overseas travel and colonization further complicated people's perspectives. Literature, art, science, and philosophy flourished as old definitions and social institutions were questioned and altered. One consequence of all of these developments and many more was a palpably increasing awareness of the self as something that was not divinely formed and statically placed, but rather changeable and possibly cultivatable through one's own concerted activity.

While the origins and inherent biases of the term "humanism" are sub-ject to considerable dispute, we can still use it to point to the Renaissance interest in such self-directed agency and the underlying "optimism about human possibilities and achievements" (Edgar and Sedgwick 1999: 180). Granted, as Tony Davies has noted, much of what we term Renaissance "humanism" is a backwards projection by nineteenth-century historians, who had their own reasons for lauding "Renaissance individualism" as it portended "the end of medieval society, with its supposedly inert aggregations of nameless, unselfconscious subjects" and the birth of "the modern nation state, populated and animated by individual citizens" (Davies 1997: 16–17). Yet when we look at a text such as Machiavelli's *The Prince* (1513), we do find a remarkably different emphasis on successful, tactical self-creation when compared to the works and ideas we discussed earlier. Machiavelli's theories of self-aware role-playing and artful manipulation were perhaps exactly what Martin Luther feared when he challenged church hierarchy and found a place (albeit a small one) for the self in the interpretation of morality. Both men were writing at precisely the same time and were part of the same challenge to traditional definitions and authorizing institutions, though in *The Prince*, the divine has no place at all. Only the classical notion of Fortune, not the Christian God, plays a role in man's life, and a limited one at that: "I believe it is probably true that fortune is the arbiter of half the things we do, leaving the other half or so to be controlled by ourselves" (Machiavelli 1999: 79). Machiavelli's purpose in *The Prince* is, of course, to detail what one should do with that half under one's own control. To the politician determined to succeed, Machiavelli counsels following self-interest above all else:

A prince . . . need not necessarily have . . . good qualities . . . , but he should certainly appear to have them. . . . He should appear to be compassionate, faithful to his word, kind, guileless, and devout. And indeed he should be so. But his disposition should be such that, if he needs to be the opposite, he knows how. You must realize this: that a prince, and especially a new prince, cannot observe all those things which give men a reputation for virtue, because in order to maintain his state he is often forced to act in defiance of good faith, of charity, of kindness, of religion. And so he should have a flexible disposition, varying as fortune and circumstances dictate. As I said above, he should not deviate from what is good, if that is possible, but he should know how to do evil, if that is necessary.

(57)

Machiavelli makes no attempt to understand human "being" in any systematic way; he is no philosopher, he is a political theorist and an opportunist. However, he does contribute to a new philosophical outlook and burgeoning belief in self-actualization, of being responsible for creating one's self in order to succeed in a changing world, and of altering that self as necessary as a context changes. In locating half of the responsibility for one's success or failure in the world in one's own ability to adapt one's self to the times and to formulate appropriate strategies for securing and maintaining power, Machiavelli points toward a form of self-consciousness and self-reflexivity that is modern in the sense of its unabashed secular pragmatism and implicit amorality. Almost four hundred years before Nietzsche, Machiavelli theorized a self-conscious "will to power" that, in the words of Quentin Skinner, elicited first "a stunned silence . . . and then a howl of execration that has never finally died away" (Skinner 2000: 42).

Other religious and political thinkers of the period were not quite so boldly secular as Machiavelli and were still attempting to conjoin self-actualization and religious belief. Focusing on this fascination with the tension between freedom and constraint, self-creation and morally responsible limitation, is perhaps the best way of engaging with the work and worldview of René Descartes. Descartes, writing in the first half of the seventeenth century and subject to all of the changes mentioned above, based his philosophical explorations of existence and truth in a process of raising doubt about that which is known and believed. In his famous fourth "Discourse on Method" (1637), he writes:

[A]s I wanted to concentrate solely on the search for truth, I thought I ought to . . . reject as being absolutely false everything in which I could suppose the slightest reason for doubt, in order to see if there did not remain after that anything in my belief which was entirely indubitable. . . . [Thus] I rejected as being false all the reasonings I had hitherto accepted as proofs. And . . . I resolved to pretend that nothing which had ever entered my mind was any more true than the illusions of my dreams. But immediately afterwards I became aware that, while I decided thus to think that everything was false, it followed necessarily that I who thought thus must be something; and observing that this truth: *I think, therefore I am*, was so certain and so evident that all the most extravagant suppositions of the skeptics were not capable of shaking it, I judged that I could accept it without scruple as the first principle of the philosophy I was seeking.

(Descartes 1968: 53–54)

While philosophers and scholars have subsequently debated whether or not Descartes's *cogito* is, in fact, indubitable, certainly the reduction of all other certitudes to this one is significant. As Garrett Thomson has noted, "Self-conscious reflection upon the sources and standards of knowledge was one of the hall-marks of the modern period. This was mostly due to Descartes. . . . He saw the need to evaluate methodically and systematically all claims to knowledge, to think about how knowledge is possible, and to reconcile the conflict between the new science and the old religion" (Thomson 2000a: 9). In Descartes's conception, thinking – really *doubting* – and struggling to know, in inevitably subjective ways, is the very basis of being. The self's apartness and individuality are central to an understanding of human *being*.

This forthright break from a philosophy of existence based on obedience to social and religious institutions and divine law led the Catholic Church to put Descartes's works on its list of banned books in 1663. Even though Descartes goes through a process of sketchy and tortured reasoning to prove God's existence in his *Meditations* (1641), his reasoning from doubt is, as Thomson observes, "clearly non-authoritarian. It liberates the individual to seek for himself or herself. In this way, it carries the spirit of a new age and is powerful politically" (Thomson 2000a: 25). T. Z. Lavine argues that by introducing the category of the subjective into philosophical understanding, Descartes opens up an almost irreparable "chasm [between his] own mind and its thoughts" and the "existence of anything else," because "subjective consciousness and its contents are separated from the physical world of nature and from the social world of human beings" (Lavine 1984: 99). Descartes's is not a philosophy without a sense of ethics, however. In fact, he suggests a supremely controlled ethics of generosity and esteem, one in which the thinking subject creates a rational mode of engagement with the world.

In relating Descartes's ideas to the mentality of the era, Taylor notes:

What one finds running through all the aspects of this constellation –

the new philosophy, methods of administration and military organization, spirit of government, and methods of discipline – is the growing ideal of a human agent who is able to remake himself by methodical and disciplined action. What this calls for is the ability to take an instrumental stance to one's given properties, desires, inclinations, tendencies, habits of thought and feeling, so that they can be *worked on*, doing away with some and strengthening others, until one meets the desired specifications. My suggestion is that Descartes's picture of the disengaged subject articulates the understanding of agency which is most congenial to this whole movement, and that is part of the grounds for its impact in his century and beyond.

(Taylor 1989: 159–60)

Indeed, an important aspect of Descartes's notion of agency – namely, *if one thinks and works hard enough, one can make oneself into a better person* – still underlies much of our thinking today about identity and our own responsibility for our selves. While we will discuss later the many qualifications of such idealized agency introduced in later centuries, especially the twentieth, even in Descartes's day it was a contested idea. The church had obvious reasons for attempting to deny subjective (even if rational) agency in the making of meaning, and to reaffirm human dependence on divine and institutional mandate. But even in the secular literature of the Renaissance, we find a palpable skepticism regarding the fully self-controlled/controllable and an intense interest in that which impedes or resists our control.

This skepticism is a theme that resonates throughout the work of Shakespeare, for instance, whose major tragedies are powerful explorations of human will and degrees of self-consciousness, and were written just a few years before Descartes's statements on those topics. Both writers were at once products of and participants in the same era of exploration regarding the question of the human ability to know and take responsibility for the self. *Hamlet* (1603) is perhaps Shakespeare's most famous exploration of selfhood and any power the thinking self possesses to change its self. Its differences from and similarities to earlier works are revealing. Like Sophocles' *Antigone*, written two thousand years earlier, the play dramatizes the tragedy caused by a self-serving ruler, Claudius, who follows his own interests and desires instead of law and tradition. But Claudius is ruthless, not simply mistaken and, taking Machiavelli's advice, he lets nothing stand in the way of his political and personal ambition. As with the earlier drama, death, destruction, and political upheaval are the tragic and edifying results of such selfish activity. But certainly the path to the righting of Claudius's wrongs is much more circuitous than was the swift response we saw to Creon's errors of judgment.

Unlike Sophocles' drama wherein the obedient Antigone is the instrument of divine retribution, Shakespeare's tragedy comes out of an age of intense reflection on selfhood and self will. While Descartes may find in thinking the very means by which he defines human being, Shakespeare reveals the limitations and drawbacks of adopting a detached, meta-conscious perspective on selfhood. Hamlet, like Antigone, knows his duty in response to the clearly unethical activity of his uncle, yet he lacks Antigone's ease of action and swift, almost mechanical, reaction. In ways unheard of during the classical era, Hamlet ponders whether the ghost of his father actually reveals the truth, he contemplates the possibility of suicide rather than forthright action, and he struggles to find motivation. To a certain extent, he is not unlike Ismene who knows but lacks the will to do her duty, but Hamlet is of course the hero of the play, whose struggles are at the center of its action. If there is an Antigone-like character in the play, it is Laertes, who moves swiftly and decisively to revenge his own father's death, but who serves only as a foil, and whose desire to act immediately without reflection and investigation is, in fact, revealed to be rash, for it is easily co-opted into Claudius's machinations.

Indeed, what makes Hamlet a hero on the cusp of the modern era is his highly self-conscious attempts to think his way into action, and to pinpoint and address deficiencies in his self. He muses, "What is a man/ If his chief good and market of his time/Be but to sleep and feed?" (Shakespeare 1992: 203). Like Descartes, Hamlet recognizes that "man" is defined by his ability to look "before and after" with "capability" and "godlike reason." But given that, he still cannot answer the question "Why yet I live to say 'This thing's to do,'/Sith I have cause, and will, and strength, and mean/To do 't" (203). Seeing many examples around him of what he *should* do, he nevertheless cannot work himself up to do anything other than think about what he should do. He even has a quasi-"self-help" philosophy that he expresses to his mother when he urges her to give up his uncle's bed: "Refrain tonight,/And that shall lend a kind of easiness to the next abstinence, the next more easy;/For use almost can change the stamp of nature" (181). But if he believes that he can reflect upon and manipulate nature by choosing to train himself differently, his own failures certainly belie the theory. He only manages to take action against his uncle in the frenzy of the play's final fight scene when he is mortally wounded, driven by emotion, not thought.

The play mocks, of course, the ease of Polonius's facile advice to Laertes: "This above all: to thine own self be true" (45), for the truth of the thinking self is that it can be paralyzed by that which defines it, thought. Also, in an era in which the surety of religion is clearly crumbling (Claudius follows his own will without real fear of divine punishment), the thinking self is further paralyzed by thoughts of what might occur after death. While Antigone fulfills her duty knowing that she will "abide" in the world of the dead forever (119), Hamlet is trapped in doubt and an actual "dread of something after death," or even worse, nothing after death. As he notes, "conscience does make cowards of us all" (129), by which he means a fearfulness deriving both from an awareness of selfhood (consciousness) and that selfhood's responsibility and often inability to determine right and wrong (our modern notion of conscience). Thus as much as Descartes in his way sees the thinking self as exercising instrumental power over selfhood, Shakespeare certainly recognized the internal war that can be waged as that self grapples with its own existential isolation. Exhilarating freedom and debilitating fear cannot be separated. And this is the quandary that philosophy and theories of identity will continue to address.

LOCKE, KANT, AND THE "WE"

As traced earlier, a profound fear of moral lawlessness attended this burgeoning recognition of freedom from religious constraints on human behavior. Philosophers therefore sought specifically secular paths to rectify human failings, and turned to "reason" as the new check on selfishness and potential moral chaos. As Edgar and Sedgwick point out in *Key Concepts in Cultural Theory*, this was the defining characteristic of what we now term the "Enlightenment," namely the eighteenth century's "faith in the ability of reason to solve social as well as intellectual and scientific problems," coupled with "an aggressively critical perspective on what were perceived as the repressive influences of tradition and institutional religion" (Edgar and Sedgwick 1999: 125–26).

Charles Taylor points to the identity theories of the British philosopher John Locke (1632–1704) as the clearest example of what was newly conceived of as the "punctual self" in the late seventeenth and eighteenth centuries. According to Taylor, Locke and his contemporaries advanced the idea, still pervasive today, that through "disengagement and rational control" the self is fully within our power to perfect. This entails first identifying discrete aspects of the self that require attention, or in other words, *objectifying* components of our *subjective* experience: "Disengagement is always correlative of an 'objectification'. . . . Objectifying a given domain involves depriving it of its normative force for us" (Taylor 1989: 160). He adds,

> Disengagement involves our going outside the first-person stance and taking on board some theory, or at least some supposition, about how things work. . . . The point of the whole operation is to gain a kind of control. Instead of being swept along to error by the ordinary bent of our experience, we stand back from it, withdraw from it, reconstrue it objectively, and then learn to draw defensible conclusions from it.
>
> (162–63)

In this way, according to Taylor, "Locke's theory generates and also reflects an ideal of independence and self-responsibility, a notion of reason as free from established custom and locally dominant authority" (167).

This ideal may seem familiar to many of us since it pervades popular psychology books even today, and is summed up well in the following call for rational self-perfection issued in Locke's *An Essay Concerning Human Understanding* (1690):

> For the mind having in most cases . . . a power to *suspend* the execution and satisfaction of any of its desires, and so all, one after another, is at liberty to consider the objects of them; examine them on all sides, and weigh them with others. In this lies the liberty Man has; and from

the not using it right comes all that variety of mistakes, errors, and faults which we run into, in the conduct of our lives; . . . To prevent this we have the power to *suspend* the prosecution of this or that desire, as every one daily may Experiment in himself. This seems to me the source of all liberty. . . . For during this *suspension* of any desire, before the *will* be determined to action, and the action (which follows the determination) be done, we have the opportunity to examine, view, and judge, of the good or evil of what we are going to do; and when, upon due *Examination*, we have judg'd, we have done our duty, all that we can, or ought to do, in pursuit of our happiness.

(Locke 1975: 263–64)

This idealization of reason may appear dry and detached, but in fact, *An Essay Concerning Human Understanding* is a work that is thoroughly imbued with optimism and an unshakable faith in human perfectibility.

Indeed, what makes it different from and preliminary to the theories of subjectivity that we will explore later is Locke's lack of sustained attention to the many and various impediments to such easy, instrumental control over the self. Subjectivity as we are exploring the critical concept here has come to comprise not only the theorization of self-awareness and the mechanics of agency over the self but also an accounting for that which impedes self-awareness and such agency. Certainly this is nascent in Locke, who recognizes for instance that we cannot will our preferences; he calls it "absurd" to imagine that "Man" can will to "be pleased with what he is pleased with" (Locke 1975: 247), or by implication at least, to will himself into different pleasures. E. J. Lowe builds significantly on Locke's implied constraints in offering a practical example: "a smoker may voluntarily undergo some sort of aversion therapy in the knowledge that at the end of it he will no longer smoke voluntarily – that is, will no longer will to smoke. But he cannot simply *will* to will not to smoke" (Lowe 1995: 134). Yet Taylor suggests that Locke would see even such limit cases as opportunities rather than fixed impediments:

Fashion and the common opinion have settled wrong notions, and education and custom ill habits, the just values of things are misplaced, and the palates of men corrupted. Pains should be taken to rectify these;

> and contrary habits change our pleasures, and give us a relish to what
> is necessary and conducive to our happiness.
>
> (Taylor 1989: 170–71)

But as Taylor would readily admit, "fashion" and "the common opinion" glance much too quickly at what we would now recognize as a complex web of beliefs, naturalized notions, biases, and entrenched valuations. Predating by two centuries the rise of psychology and the other social sciences, Locke has neither the vocabulary nor the inclination to analyze how those wrong notions become settled and to what extent they are difficult, if not impossible to unsettle, especially when generally held to be true. Indeed, we would recognize today that notions are often wrong because they affect people differentially, categorize them in ways that can oppress (mentally and materially), and make wholly unrealistic the possibility of instrumental control. What Locke ignores is that access to the resources (educational, therapeutic, even economic or domestic) abetting any type of control is limited to a very few people. To this extent, his theories of identity are not at all politicized.

However, Locke certainly was an expressly political theorist and many of his ideals of instrumental control over the self linger as ours. Also, his ideals of political rights and tolerance continue as motivational forces still driving some of our struggles in the realm of identity politics. Locke's is the quintessential liberal political perspective. In his *Treatises on Government* (1689) he emphasizes government's role in assuring a level playing field in which society's participants have the ability to work toward and achieve the rational self-perfection mentioned above. Furthermore, he allows that governments unwilling or unable to meet the needs of the majority of their citizens are subject to legitimate revolutionary change (although in emphasizing always the majority he does ignore the problem of minorities oppressed by the majority). As many commentators have pointed out, this emphasis on political agency was reflected in Locke's own participation in the Glorious Revolution of 1688–89 in which the despotic James II was deposed and replaced by William III, who accepted the Bill of Rights and Parliament's primacy in government. Here as earlier, Locke helped lay the groundwork for certain ideals of equality, tolerance, and justice that still play a major part in our debates today on the interplay of individual identity and politics, even as his discussion of what *should be* glances only obliquely at that which limits our ability to realize our ideals.

Yet Locke's was only one voice in a wide-ranging conversation during this era. Immanuel Kant (1724–1804) also desired to articulate a set of new ideals concerning human activity and interpersonal responsibility; this is the portion of his highly complex theories of knowledge and experience that is most pertinent to our discussion here. In response to the thorough skepticism of David Hume (1711–76), who questioned philosophy's ability to generate any hard-and-fast laws, Kant defended the ability of reason to decide between right and wrong, and even to construct inviolable, universal law. Though differing from Locke in many respects, Kant reaffirms the concept of the rational agent, whose primary duty is to bring selfish personal desires and behaviors into line with reason-based ideals of social duty.

Kant's own approach to the complex question of self-consciousness and limits on human agency is, in fact, to simplify the discussion (though in notoriously difficult language). As Garrett Thomson notes:

> The Rationalist Descartes takes the "I think" to indicate the existence of a substance distinct from the body. This ignores an important paradox concerning consciousness – which is that we cannot experience it because it is experience. Hence, the saying "the I which sees cannot see itself." Kant recognizes this paradoxical point and explains it. According to him, the "I" is not an object of possible experience, because it is a presupposition of experience. Kant does not treat the I as a thing.
>
> (Thomson 2000b: 13)

In other words, "the search for the 'I' is pointless, because any seeking must be done by the 'I' and so what is sought is already presupposed" (Thomson 2000b: 55). By excluding from consideration the "search for the 'I'," Kant is then able to suggest that rational human behavior can be reduced to a single ethical principle: the categorical imperative.

In fact, Kant argues that *subjectivity* and *objectivity* are coextensive (or should be, in theory). In his *Fundamental Principles of the Metaphysics of Morals* (1785), he establishes that fact firmly before he articulates his ethical imperative:

> Now an action done from duty must wholly exclude the influence of inclination, and with it every object of the will, so that nothing remains which can determine the will except objectively the *law*, and subjectively *pure respect* for this practical law, and consequently the maxim that I should follow this law even to the thwarting of all my inclinations.
>
> (Kant 2001: 159)

He glosses the above statement with the explanation that a maxim "is the subjective principle of volition. The objective principle (*i.e.* that which would also serve subjectively as a practical example to all rational beings if reason had full power over the faculty of desire) is the practical *law*" (159). Clarifying the situation thereby, he then lays down his firm imperative reinforcing the link between subjective and objective activity: "I am never to act otherwise than so *that I could also will that my maxim should become a universal law*" (160). While Kant will go on to explain that it is also imperative that we should create conditions under which all persons can exercise their free will in this way, he does finally hold all individuals accountable for their strict adherence to this notion of duty, even if others do not. Thus as Karl Jaspers notes, "Extraordinarily drastic statements may be found in Kant" (Jaspers 1962: 71), whose imperative would not even allow for a lie that one might tell to protect oneself from wildly unethical actions by criminals or despots.

Furthermore, Kant wholly ignores the many presuppositions that may go into any decision that a given action *should* be a universal law. His own blind spots are easy for us to see from the perspective of over two centuries. Kant, as a product of his era, was unequivocally sexist and to his mind women were by definition irrational beings. As this was an incontrovertible fact for Kant, his categorical imperative would allow for the rigid exclusion of women from the educational system and political realm. Similarly, Kant, who was solitary and celibate in his own life, was convinced that sexual activity was, again categorically, for procreation alone, and as Roger Sullivan notes, it was unquestionably "immoral to frustrate that purpose deliberately" (Sullivan 1994: 157). Non-procreative sexualities, whether heterosexual or homosexual, were categorically excluded from ethical defense or justification. Thus it is clear that Kant's "universalities" were only those of a particular time, place, and social position. This is not to point a finger of blame at Kant, but it does demonstrate how different our notions of identity are today, and how much was left unaccounted for in Kant's theories, even if he also articulates still widely recognized rules of mutual respect and one's inherent right to pursue happiness, so long as the happiness of others is not jeopardized. In those ways, Kant does begin to lay the groundwork for later theories of *inter*-subjectivity in his calls for sympathy and respect (within the limits mentioned above); this made him of continuing interest to twentieth-century commentators such as Hannah Arendt and Seyla Benhabib. Yet certainly there is no allowance in Kant that different material circumstances, cultural contexts, legacies, and/or language systems might create strikingly different moralities and universalities. Kant lived a rigidly disciplined daily life and was an equally hard taskmaster in his philosophical injunctions. Indeed, one reason that his views have warranted sustained attention here is that his universalizing tendencies are mirrored today in the "common sense" rejoinders of those who would reduce discussions of agency and the interplay of the text of the self and its meaning-making context to non-questions or ones answered simply with objectively based maxims.

In fact, Kant even seems rigid and overly self-confident vis-à-vis the imaginative literature of the seventeenth and eighteenth centuries, which was much more attuned to the complex cultural/subcultural specificity involved in the generation of moral law and the many subjective constraints on people's ability to know and do right as objectively determined. We might even think of this exploration of ambiguity as a defining characteristic of the great satires of the era. In *Gulliver's Travels* (1726), for example, Jonathan Swift uses his exaggerated representations of the Lilliputians, the Laputans, and the Yahoos to ridicule the varieties of self-importance and other vices of his day. Yet at the same time, his supremely rational Houyhnhnms, whose "grand Maxim is, to cultivate *Reason*, and to be wholly governed by it" (Swift 1998: 259), are equally inappropriate as role models for his hero Gulliver. Gulliver's pride and misanthropy at the end of his narrative are shocking, even if he is self-consciously attempting to live a life of reason. What Gulliver loses is his ability to understand the reasons accounting for the failings of others, to love his wife and children in spite of their imperfections, and to find ways of comprehending human complexity and differences outside of a rigid Houyhnhnm/Yahoo binary. Indeed, the Houyhnhnms cannot even comprehend the word "opinion" since reason for them is not "a Point problematical as with us, where Men can argue with Plausibility on both Sides of a Question; but strikes you with immediate Conviction; as it must needs do where it is not mingled, obscured, or discoloured by Passion or Interest" (259). Yet even if that stance means that "Controversies, Wranglings, Disputes, and Positiveness in false or dubious Propositions, are Evils unknown among the *Houyhnhnms*" (260), its starkness and anti-dialogic nature leads to smugness, stasis, and isolation in Gulliver himself, who at the end of the narrative is only comfortable among his horses and cannot bear the touch of another human being. The book as a whole cautions us to allow our perspectives to shift and our knowledge of variability and human imperfection to unsettle our certainties, even those seemingly dictated by pure reason.

Satire thus demands a double (if not multi-layered) consciousness in which the audience knows well the ideal rules of social interaction, morality, and genre (or whatever other convention is being satirized) yet is also able to immerse itself in the exaggerated, skewed, or flawed system of reference within the satire. To be sure, satire is often conservative in that it seeks through its highlighting of hypocrisy or rank corruption a return to some purer or more consistent form of morality. Even then, however, it does demonstrate that individuals and groups are discrete elements within society who often generate their own moral systems, ones with highly developed, internally consistent rules and justifications, and that are quite understandable as micro-systems of subjective adoption and interrogation of broader social rules. This consciousness of self-interested, subcultural participation in and response to a larger context of social corruption will be a key component of nineteenth- and twentieth-century theories of politicized subjectivity.

This helps to explain why John Gay's *The Beggar's Opera* (1728) continues to be revisited and updated to meet the needs of new audiences and critique a variety of political contexts. But even in its first mani-festation as a successful stage production in London, it both reflected and reinforced its audience's ability to place the corrupt activities of its underworld characters within the larger corrupt socio-political system of its day. In later versions by Bertolt Brecht and Vaclav Havel, the play's broad social critique is refined and adapted, but class consciousness is certainly emergent even in Gay's prototype. In the play's opening aria, Peachum sings and then opines:

> Through all the employments of life,
>   Each neighbor abuses his brother;
> Whore and rogue they call husband and wife:
>   All professions be-rogue one another.
> The priest calls the lawyer a cheat,
>   The lawyer be-knaves the divine;
> And the statesman, because he's so great,
>   Thinks his trade as honest as mine.
> A lawyer is an honest employment; so is mine. Like me, too, he acts in a double capacity, both against rogues and for 'em; for 'tis fitting that we should protect and encourage cheats, since we live by them.
>
> (Gay 1979: 188)

The play implies that with corruption so pervasive, Peachum's adherence to the general moral dynamic of his times may make him theoretically culpable but certainly practical and pragmatic at the same time; indeed, the criminals of the play style themselves "practical philosophers" (207). In their view, an idealized ethics divergent from that of the general society would be absurd. And as Mrs. Peachum argues with her daughter Polly over whether she has been "ruined" by marrying Macheath and whether or not she will do her "duty" by hanging her husband, we find that language and moral law are emptied wholly of their fixed and traditional values. If Kant puts his faith, theoretically, in the collapse of subjectivity and objectivity into internalized maxims, that term as it appears in Gay's play ("It hath always been my maxim, that one friend should assist another" [237]) signals a state in which moral laws are created in wholly contingent fashion. This dynamic may be exaggerated in Gay's dramatization of the activities of thieves, but it is reflective of a broad dynamic and set of social anxieties. Depraved contexts, it is feared, create depraved subjects, and those contexts are the specific interests and targets of many nineteenth-century theories of subjectivity in its real life messiness and thorough moral ambiguity.

2

THE NINETEENTH AND EARLY TWENTIETH CENTURIES

SLAVERY AND SUBJECTIVITIES

In turning now to the ways discussions of subjectivity became explicitly politicized as we move into and through the nineteenth century, there are any number of more or less contemporaneous activities that could serve as our first example. The French Revolution of 1789 was an event of unparalleled magnitude as it signaled a dramatically expanding consciousness of class oppression and the causes and consequences of violent revolution. At roughly the same time, a small but vocal group of women began to question openly the norms of gender identity and the social beliefs justifying the prejudicial treatment of one half of humankind. But perhaps no single issue more clearly demonstrates the terrible omissions in, and need for, forthright challenges to early modern and Enlightenment theories of subjectivity than that of slavery and the continuing devaluation of groups of people on the basis of their race. As we saw with Kant's categorical exclusion of women from certain sectors of social activity, universal claims regarding personhood and interpersonal responsibility often reflect deep-seated biases and can contain significant and shocking exceptions.

Many theorists of subjectivity largely ignored the issue of race, even during the twentieth century. For Jacques Lacan, Louis Althusser, and Michel Foucault, whose work we will discuss later, race is a tangential topic, when it is mentioned at all. Even Charles Taylor's *Sources of the Self*, as detailed and impressively researched as it is, mentions race only briefly. He states that in the past two centuries the "language of subjective rights" has "steadily eroded hierarchy and promoted equality . . . in all sorts of dimensions, between social classes, races, ethnic and cultural groups, and the sexes" (Taylor 1989: 395). He also points out that in a statement from

> 1823, the recently founded Liverpool Society for the Abolition of Slavery attributed its unprecedented success in achieving moral "improvement" to the "practice of combining society itself in intellectual masses, for the purpose of attaining some certain, defined, and acknowledged good, which is generally allowed to be essential to the well-being of the whole."
>
> (396)

That consciousness of the efficacy of mass organization is certainly important to note. But the larger issue at stake in abolitionist movements of the late eighteenth and nineteenth centuries was who, in fact, was even worthy of consideration as human and in full possession of the self-awareness, rights, and responsibilities ascribed to the subject of so much philosophical speculation. And, as we will see here and in later sections, a key component of that debate was the effect of groups beginning to speak on behalf of themselves rather than have their interests and perspectives articulated by others.

Certainly the perspectives on race of all of the supposedly enlightened philosophers discussed earlier were highly tendentious and often blatantly self-interested. As vocal as he was about desiring to create a level playing field for all participants in the political arena, John Locke also "profited from slave trade, justified slavery in his writings, codified it in the constitutions he wrote for American colonies, advocated colonial conquest, and denied the right to rebel against the colonial power" (Andrew 1988: 62). Henry Louis Gates notes that David Hume, a thorough skeptic concerning philosophy's ability to pronounce *any* universal truths, did venture the following pronouncement: "I am apt to suspect the Negroes, and in general all the other species of men (for there are four or five different kinds) to be naturally inferior to whites" (cit. Gates 1985a: 10). Kant, Gates goes on to demonstrate, was in fact "one of the earliest major European philosophers to conflate color with intelligence" (10). Gates finds in Kant's *Observations on the Feeling of the Beautiful and Sublime* (1764) a categorical rejection of the statements of a "Negro carpenter" because "'this fellow was *quite black* from head to foot, a clear proof that what he said was stupid.' The correlation of 'black' and 'stupid' Kant posits as if it were self-evident," Gates concludes (10–11). All of this and more, Gates argues, reveals "the remarkable capacity of European philosophers to conceive of 'humanity' in ideal terms (white, male) yet despise, abhor, colonize, or exploit human beings who are not 'ideal'" (Gates 1985b: 408).

In the deepening social dialogue on slavery and the slave trade, this hypocrisy gradually came to the foreground. In Aphra Behn's *Oroonoko, or The Royal Slave* from 1688, we find a moving fictional biography of a "gallant slave" (Behn 2000: 2,171) who, before he is taken by traders, is described in ways meant to challenge contemporary prejudices:

> Nor did the perfections of his mind come short of those of his person, for his discourse was admirable upon almost any subject; and whoever had heard him speak would have been convinced of their errors, that all fine wit is confined to the white men, especially those of Christendom, and would have confessed that Oroonoko was as capable even of reigning well, and of governing as wisely, had as great a soul, as politic maxims, and was as sensible of power, as any prince civilized in the most refined schools of humanity and learning, or the most illustrious courts.
>
> (2,175)

Oroonoko retains those noble attributes even in servitude, and finally dies a martyr's death in the colony of Surinam. In emphasizing Oroonoko's heroic qualities, Behn clearly repudiates racist restrictions on who falls within the category of human and deserves all of the rights and considerations that Locke, for example, was theorizing as fundamental to white human being.

Yet a vital consideration in exploring the interplay of race and subjectivity was the effect of racism on the interior sense of selfhood of the oppressed, and as insightful as Behn was, this is a topic that cannot be spoken about authoritatively from outside of the affected group, however well intentioned the social critic or theorist might be. Even as abolitionist groups formed in England in the mid- to late eighteenth century and pressed the government to outlaw slavery (which was achieved in 1772) and English participation in the slave trade (finally achieved in 1807), Parliamentary debates and journalistic polemics could do little to capture the complexity of slavery's violent objectification of human subjects, without the addition of the actual voices and perspectives of the affected individuals themselves. Those voices gradually emerged. Ignatius Sancho (1729–80) was born a slave but became well educated as a butler to the Duke of Montague; he wrote a series of letters to contemporaries on the subject of slavery that were published posthumously in 1782. In one to Jack Wingrave, who had written of his disgust for the "blacks" in India, Sancho speaks of how the selfhoods of "simple, harmless people" of colonized places were deformed through the activities of ruthless and greedy colonizers, so "that the poor ignorant natives soon learnt to turn the knavish and diabolical arts – which they too soon imbibed – upon their teacher" (Sancho 2000: 2,810). As condescending toward those native peoples as this remark may seem, we do find in it, over two centuries ago, a unique insight into the subjectivities of the oppressed, who learn to use the tactics of their oppressors against the interests of the empowered group and who come to live a hybrid existence that intermingles traditional with aspects of colonial culture. Indeed, Sancho's nascent theory of social construction, hybridity, and tactical response will resurface as a key component of twentieth-century theories of subjectivity that we will consider later. Sancho ends his letter by stating:

> But enough – it is a subject that sours my blood – and I am sure will not please the friendly bent of your social affections. – I mentioned these only to guard my friend against being too hasty in condemning

the knavery of a people who, bad as they may be – possibly – were made worse by their Christian visitors.

(2,810)

These are some of the first expressions we have of the effect of objectification on the subjectivity of oppressed peoples, and are a still powerful critique of the hypocrisies of self-styled agents of civilization.

What the English publication of Sancho's letters, as well as that of autobiographical writings by the former slaves Olaudah Equiano (c.1745–97) and Mary Prince (c.1788–c.1833), helped demonstrate was that contemporary theories of identity, self-cultivation, and self-actualization were far from universal, for they still concerned only the rights, roles, and responsibilities of a relatively few individuals of privilege. This is certainly clear in the theory behind and practice of democracy in the United States. As explicitly as the "Declaration of Independence" from 1776 stated as "self-evident Truths" that "all Men are created equal, that they are endowed by their Creator with certain unalienable Rights, that among these are Life, Liberty, and the Pursuit of Happiness," one charge the same document leveled against George III was that he "has excited domestic Insurrections amongst us, and endeavoured to bring on the Inhabitants of our Frontiers, the merciless Indian Savages, whose known Rule of Warfare, is an undistinguished Destruction, of all Ages, Sexes and Conditions" (Jefferson 1975: 238). Native Americans and, of course, slaves were categorically excluded from the group of "Men" with unalienable rights. Different and more nuanced theories of subjectivity were needed to account for how such naturalized degradation affected the self-identities of individuals long denied access to economic resources, political rights, education, and even basic recognition as rational, capable human beings.

As we will see in Chapter 3, late twentieth-century theorists of race and postcoloniality discuss such dynamics at great length, but certainly the voices of abolitionists, former slaves, and early Black commentators on racism in the United States offered significant insights during the nineteenth and early twentieth centuries. In *Narrative of the Life of Frederick Douglass* (1845), Douglass (c.1817–95) speaks powerfully of the daily horrors of slave existence, and also of the effect of slavery on the very selfhoods of the enslaved. Like Sancho above, Douglass reveals the necessary adoption of tactical dissembling among slaves in order for them to exist and protect themselves:

> The slaveholders have been known to send in spies among their slaves, to ascertain their views and feelings in regard to their condition. The frequency of this has had the effect to establish among the slaves the maxim, that a still tongue makes a wise head. They suppress the truth rather than take the consequences of telling it.
>
> (Douglass 1973: 20)

This is a maxim far different from that promoted by Kant, though not far afield from those of Gay's characters, as Douglass explores contextual influences and powerful constraints on any notion of idealized human identity and day-to-day behavior. And Douglass is equally incisive in examining the effects on masters of the power allowed over slaves. Even those who assume their slaveholding responsibilities with some measure of kindness and consideration are soon wholly corrupted:

> My new mistress . . . had been in a good degree preserved from the blighting and dehumanizing effects of slavery. I was utterly astonished at her goodness. . . . But, alas! This kind heart had but a short time to remain such. The fatal poison of irresponsible power was already in her hands, and soon commenced its infernal work. That cheerful eye, under the influence of slavery, soon became red with rage; that voice, made all of sweet accord, changed to one of harsh and horrid discord; and that angelic face gave place to that of a demon.
>
> (35–36)

In ways unimaginable for white, privileged, Anglo-European philosophers, Douglass had an ability to trace the micro-physics of unchecked power on the subjectivities of oppressors and the oppressed. Harriet Jacobs (1813–97) is similarly eloquent in her *Incidents in the Life of a Slave Girl* (1861) in discussing how "slavery is a curse to the whites as well as to the blacks" (Jacobs 2000: 56), in deforming both groups' subjectivities. Jacobs's and Douglass's experiential bases allowed them insights unavailable to Kant, Locke, and others. Indeed, with these writers and their contemporaries we find one of the birthplaces of identity politics as we know it today.

But before we move onto other, contemporaneous origins of theories of marginalized and potentially politicizable subjectivities, it is important to recognize the most important early philosopher examining the lingering effects of slavery and impact of continuing racism on the psyches and self-conceptions of African-Americans. W. E. B. Du Bois (1868–1963) was well acquainted with the history of philosophical discussions of identity, agency, and ethics when he published *The Souls of Black Folk* in 1903. In it, he asks and painstakingly answers the question "How does it feel to be a problem?" (Du Bois 1989: 1), by which he means a member of a group long oppressed, still suffering the effects of that oppression, and yet judged by external standards of conduct and self-actualization that wholly ignore the force of oppression. He speaks from the perspective of a man

> born in a world which yields him no true self-consciousness, but only lets him see himself through the revelation of the other world. It is a peculiar sensation, this double-consciousness, this sense of always looking at one's self through the eyes of others, of measuring one's soul by the tape of a world that looks on in amused contempt and pity. One ever feels his twoness, – an American, a Negro, two souls, two thoughts, two unreconciled strivings; two warring ideals in one dark body, whose dogged strength alone keeps it from being torn asunder.
>
> The history of the American Negro is the history of this strife, – this longing to attain self-conscious manhood, to merge this double self into a better and truer self.
>
> (3)

In saying that he wants to retain both of his identities – as an African and an American – Du Bois is one of the first theorists of multiple subject positions; he recognizes that identity for many people is not a perfectly seamless whole, but hyphenated and at times internally contestatory, even as the desire for internal integration and wholeness may remain the elusive ideal. Yet, he suggests, "a double life, with double thoughts, double duties, and double social classes, must give rise to double words and double ideals, and tempt the mind to pretence or revolt, to hypocrisy or radicalism" (142). Indeed, there are no easy answers to the problems generated by long-standing violence perpetrated against selfhood, only, in Du Bois's opinion, very gradual healing through education and consciousness raising, and very halting processes of self-recovery. Those processes are very slow, indeed, and the horrible legacy of slavery and its impact on subjectivity linger to this day on the African continent, in the USA, and across the globe.

WOLLSTONECRAFT AND EARLY FEMINIST SUBJECTIVITY

The same mindset of burgeoning challenge to tradition, and especially to traditional definitions of who falls within the category of "human" and is the recipient of all of the rights conferred thereby, accounts for the stirrings of feminist consciousness during the eighteenth century. In fact, the writings of the philosophers of the Enlightenment provided very fertile ground for feminist thought and response. As Alice Browne notes in *The Eighteenth Century Feminist Mind,*

> Locke does not say a great deal about women, but what he says does not rule out the possibility of extending citizens' rights to women. . . .
> By basing political power on contract, and arguing against the notion that it derives from a divinely instituted patriarchal power traceable back to Adam, he removes one of the principle arguments for men's power over women.
>
> (Browne 1987: 20)

But Locke was not the only male philosopher of the era whose theories concerned women's roles and rights, and one in particular, Jean-Jacques Rousseau (1712–78), stirred a great deal of controversy. While Rousseau's was a highly conservative voice on gender, arguing for naturally separate spheres for men and women, Browne makes the point that

> Locke's views could fit in with the side of eighteenth-century feminist thought which emphasized women's likeness to men, while Rousseau's could provide inspiration for feminists who emphasized women's separate and special needs. . . . Rousseau's work encouraged women's

> sense of themselves as a group in society with rights and duties defined
> by their gender.
>
> (20–21)

Indeed, that debate between theorists emphasizing sameness and others emphasizing difference between the sexes will reach a fever pitch in twentieth-century discussions of gender roles and rights. But the more important immediate effect of Rousseau's insistence on women's solely domestic/maternal nature in *Emile* (1762) and other works, was the stark contrast such conservatism provided with his otherwise radical statements on the natural equality of all men and the corruption of social institutions that inhibit freedom of thought. Indeed, key to an understanding of the changing nature of subjectivity as we are discussing the concept here, is how conceptions of the self have metamorphosed over time with reference, and in response to, changing economic and material conditions, and also a host of newly recognizable/recognized bigotries, social inequities, and hypocrisies. Without Rousseau's articulation of a blatant double standard, Mary Wollstonecraft (1759–97) would not have had a clear target for her powerful condemnation of hypocritical gender norms in her *Vindication of the Rights of Woman* (1792). As we will see later in our discussion of Michel Foucault's theory of the "tactical polyvalence of discourse," an "instrument of power" – such as Rousseau's – can thus serve as a useful "starting point for an opposing strategy" (Foucault 1990: 102).

Wollstonecraft's response to Rousseau is not without its own troubling aspects; as David Glover and Cora Kaplan point out in *Genders*, her ideal for women is more or less the "eighteenth-century ideal of masculinity" (Glover and Kaplan 2000: 49). However, Wollstonecraft is certainly remarkable in her firm insistence on the socially constructed nature of gender and her painstaking analysis of the impact of social oppression on the very selfhoods of women. Her departure from Rousseau is explicit: "'Educate women like men,' says Rousseau, 'and the more they resemble our sex the less power will they have over us.' This is the very point I aim at. I do not wish them to have power over men; but over themselves" (Wollstonecraft 1988: 62). Taking Rousseau's own revolutionary point concerning the corrupting effects of modern society, she turns it to her own ends, specifically targeting contemporary norms of socialization for women: "Novels, music, poetry, and gallantry, all tend to make women the creatures of sensation, and their character is thus formed in the mould of folly" (61). She continues, "the whole tenour of female education (the education of society) tends to render the best disposed romantic and inconstant; and the remainder vain and mean" (75).

Like that of the commentators on race quoted above, hers is a new perspective on marginalized subjectivity from the inside of oppression, though admittedly from a position of economic privilege as well. She takes Rousseau's theories and criticism of socialization processes and uses his own concepts to account for the very behavior that he takes as evidence of and justification for separate spheres. Thus she traces acutely the tactical maneuverings of a social group whose activities are relegated to "the little incidents of the day" and whose members "necessarily grow up cunning":

> My very soul has often sickened at observing the sly tricks practised by women to gain some foolish thing on which their silly hearts are set. Not allowed to dispose of money or call any thing their own, they learn to turn the market penny; or, should a husband offend, by staying from home, or give rise to some emotions of jealousy – a new gown, or any pretty bawble, smooths Juno's angry brow.
>
> (169)

She sums up her argument at the end of the book:

> Asserting the rights which women in common with men ought to contend for, I have not attempted to extenuate their faults; but to prove them to be the natural consequence of their education and station in society. If so, it is reasonable to suppose that they will change their character, and correct their vices and follies, when they are allowed to be free in a physical, moral, and civil sense.
>
> (194)

Granted, what Wollstonecraft is calling for here is the admission of women into the group allowed to exercise the punctual control over selfhood already theorized as available to men of the era: "I wish to see my sex become more like moral agents" (178), she insists. However, this is no small re-theorization of subjectivity. She asserts broadly that by challenging traditional social definitions and by altering socialization processes, selfhood itself becomes highly malleable. Thus Wollstonecraft dramatically augments Locke's notion of self-responsibility and self-control, for she insists that key to asserting such power over the self is the need to expose and rectify biases inherent in language, education, and underlying categories of thought. Wollstonecraft is thus one of our first theorists of social constructionism.

She was followed soon by others, who continued her exploration of the interplay of contextual constraints on, and inherent potential for, self-responsibility and self-aware agency among women. The nineteenth and early twentieth centuries saw the first theorization and growing influence of what we now term "liberal" feminist thought, which, as Rosemarie Tong suggests, continues to underlie the thinking of groups such as the National Organization for Women in the United States, in asserting that:

> female subordination is rooted in a set of customary and legal constraints that blocks women's entrance and success in the so-called public world. Because society has the belief that women are, by nature, less intellectually and/or physically capable than men, it excludes women from the academy, the forum, and the marketplace. As a result of this policy of exclusion, the true potential of many women goes unfulfilled.
>
> (Tong 1989: 2)

Tong notes that the "liberal" answer to this long history of deprivation is "first, to make the rules of the game fair and, second, to make certain that none of the runners in the race for society's goods and services is systemically disadvantaged" (2). But as Ruth Robbins points out in *Literary Feminisms*, "liberal feminists sometimes forget that their allegiance to the liberal individual is also an allegiance with competitive capitalist economics, and that wherever there is competition, there are losers as well as winners" (Robbins 2000: 25).

Yet even with that important caveat, it is vital to recognize that the early theorists of liberal feminism offered dramatic new insight into women's sense of selfhood, as they focused specifically on the internal aspects of/deformations caused by women's existence "under" patriarchy.

Like Wollstonecraft, the American Transcendentalist Margaret Fuller (1810–50) in *Woman in the Nineteenth Century* (1845) traces the causes and consequences of women's state of degraded subjectivity, as she urges her female readership to be defiantly "self-centred," never to be "absorbed by any relation" (Fuller 1971: 176). By this she does not mean that women should be "selfish," rather she urges their "self-subsistence in its two forms of self-reliance and self-impulse" (175). Women, she insists, "must leave off asking [men] and being influenced by them, but retire within themselves, and explore the ground-work of life till they find their peculiar secret" (121). Until that happens, she concludes, "there is no woman, only an overgrown child" (176). Indeed, only by following a regimen that appears almost a form of strength-training in independent selfhood – the mental equivalent of "[c]old bathing and exercise," an "inward baptism" coupled with "noble, exhilarating employment for the thoughts and the passion" (139) – can such a process of re-creating the self occur when women have always already been (de)formed by powerful socialization processes.

While many of Fuller's exhortations were preoccupied with that internal transformation process, those of her contemporaries Harriet Taylor Mill (1807–58) and John Stuart Mill (1806–73) were much more institutionally directed. Theirs is a thoroughly pragmatic perspective, grounded firmly in a liberal political faith in "access"-based solutions to deep-seated social problems. In "The Enfranchisement of Women" (1851) Harriet Taylor Mill argues that women will be able to attain full rational self-realization once they are allowed:

1 *Education* in primary and high schools, universities, medical, legal, and theological institutions.
2 *Partnership* in the labors and gains, risks, and remunerations of productive industry.
3 A *coequal share* in the formation and administration of laws – municipal, state, and national – through legislative assemblies, courts, and executive officers.

(Mill 1970: 95)

In "The Subjection of Women" (1869) John Stuart Mill turns to existing constraints on women's self-realization, generating in effect a theory of subjectivity that explores the connection between subjection, "the legal subordination of one sex to the other," and selfhood, though still with the express faith that the answer to the ills of gendered society lies in replacing the "existing social relations between the sexes" with a "principle of perfect equality" (Mill 1975: 427).

Yet even if this remedy may seem suspiciously simple to us, certainly Mill's insights into women's subjected selfhood are profound. In responding to the observation that the "rule of men over women . . . is accepted voluntarily; women make no complaint, and are consenting parties to it" (442), he notes that "All causes, social and natural, combine to make it unlikely that women should be collectively rebellious to the power of men" (443). Women are "strenuously taught to repress [all aspirations] as contrary to the proprieties of their sex" (442). Men have "put everything in practice to enslave" the minds of women:

> The masters of all other slaves rely, for maintaining obedience, on fear; either fear of themselves, or religious fears. The masters of women wanted more than simple obedience, and they turned the whole force of education to effect their purpose. All women are brought up from the very earliest years in the belief that their ideal of character is the very opposite to that of men; not self-will, and government by self-control, but submission, and yielding to the control of others.
>
> (444)

Writing at the time of the birth of the social sciences, Mill claims that the most "important department of psychology" is an "analytic study of . . . the laws of the influence of circumstances on character" (453). Noting that "[w]e cannot isolate a human being from the circumstances of his condition, so as to ascertain experimentally what he would have been by nature," he does maintain that "we can consider what he is, and what his circumstances have been, and whether the one would have been capable of producing the other" (507). Mill's interest in that "life of subjection to the will of others" (542) is one that continues to be central to investigations of selfhood and agency even today.

Yet as we saw earlier with theorists examining the effects of racism on the psyche of the oppressor, Mill is also fascinated by the subjectivity of the empowered, of the boy who grow[s] up to manhood in the belief that without any merit or exertion of his own, though he may be the most frivolous and empty or the most ignorant and stolid of mankind, by the mere fact of being born a male he is by right the superior of all and every one of an entire half of the human race: including probably some whose real superiority to himself he has daily or hourly occasion to feel.

(523)

This, he argues, "pervert[s] the whole manner of existence of the man, both as an individual and as a social being" (523). However, Mill continues to hold out tremendous optimism that through legal/institutional changes, the perversion of both sexes' subjectivities can be redressed:

For what is the peculiar character of the modern world – the difference which chiefly distinguishes modern institutions, modern social ideas, modern life itself, from those of times long past? It is, that human beings are no longer born to their place in life, and chained down by an inexorable bond to the place they are born to, but are free to employ their faculties, and such favourable chances as offer, to achieve the lot which may appear to them most desirable.

(445)

Following Locke and the other philosophers of the Enlightenment, Mill believes that extending such instrumental control over selfhood and abetting "the unfettered choice of individuals" (446) to make what they will of themselves is the means by which society improves itself; ensuring "freedom of individual choice" (447) is thus the guiding principle of his social theory.

But if feminist social philosophy of the nineteenth century remained idealistic in its conceptualization of the possibility for fully instrumental control over and enactment of selfhood, the literature of the era certainly lingered in the human struggles, limitations, and naturalized constraints that are the mundane matter of subjectivity. Women writers of the era who might have agreed with the ultimate aims of Wollstonecraft's, Fuller's, and the Mills' socio-political theories still recognized and rendered in their novels the murkiness and morass of interior life among the "subjected."

Charlotte Bronte's heroine in *Jane Eyre* (1847), whatever her theoretical potential, must live her life within a social system of gender and class oppression that leaves her few options for exercising choice over her enactment of selfhood. In one famous scene Jane recognizes and decides to work within these limitations, as she prepares to leave Lowood, her childhood school and place of employment:

> school-rules, school-duties, school-habits and notions, and voices, and faces, and phrases, and costumes, and preferences, and antipathies: such was what I knew of existence. And now I felt that it was not enough: I tired of the routine of eight years in one afternoon. I desired liberty, for liberty I gasped; for liberty I uttered a prayer; it seemed scattered on the wind then faintly blowing. I abandoned it and framed a humbler supplication; for change, stimulus: that petition, too, seemed swept off into vague space: "Then," I cried, half desperate, "grant me at least a new servitude!"
>
> (Bronte 1982: 88)

That ability to "serve elsewhere," she comes to recognize, is the extent to which she can "get [her] own will" given her gender, her familial and economic situation, and the many other contextual constraints she encounters (88). While later she comes to recognize that she always has the ability to say "no" to an oppressive situation, to choose flight, even possibly death, over immorality, there and elsewhere her subjective processing of her own degrees of agency provides some of the most compelling intellectual content of the novel. *Jane Eyre* and many of the other great novels by women writers of the Victorian era thus explore the micro-level negotiations conducted by women whose inner lives are portrayed for readers and are revealed in all of the complexity of compromised agency and aspirations unrealized, or realized and found unfulfilling.

That investigation of women's subjectivity within a patriarchal context is the primary subject matter of much of George Eliot's work. Eliot anticipates some of the complex interests of her novels of the 1860s and 1870s in an essay from 1855 entitled "Margaret Fuller and Mary Wollstonecraft" in which she praises both writers for their realistic assessment of the effect of current restrictions and their imagining of future potentials. She shares their broad perspective on subjectivity in suggesting that there "is a perpetual action and reaction between individuals and institutions; we must try and mend both by little and little – the only way in which human things can be mended" (Eliot 1992a: 185). Above all, she appreciates Fuller's and Wollstonecraft's lack of "sentimental exaggeration" (186) concerning women's current subjective state given men's "reluctance to encourage self-help and independent resources in women" (185).

Yet while that context of deprivation is always acknowledged as the primary explanation for the creation of what she terms "ignorant and feeble-minded women" (181), here and elsewhere Eliot also registers her own exasperation with such women, seeming to acknowledge their social construction but stopping short of admitting any form or degree of social determination that would mitigate their primary self-responsibility. In her scathing assessment of much popular fiction written by women, "Silly Novels by Lady Novelists" (1856), she asserts, "Society is a very culpable entity, and has to answer for the manufacture of many unwhole-some commodities, from bad pickles to bad poetry. But society . . . has its share of excessive blame as well as excessive praise" (Eliot 1992b: 320). Indeed, she points her own finger of blame for bad writing by women squarely at the women writers themselves: "In the majority of women's books you see that kind of facility which springs from the absence of any high standard; that fertility in imbecile combination or feeble imitation which a little self-criticism would check and reduce to barrenness" (319). These are harsh words, but we should recognize that Eliot speaks here and elsewhere with all the frustration of a member of an oppressed group who, even as she understands the effects of oppression, also wants to dissociate herself from others acting in what we might term "stereotypical" fashion. As a highly disciplined intellectual and soon-to-be serious novelist, she has little real interest in the compromised subjectivity of the writers of "silly novels," holding them to a requirement for "self-criticism" that is implicitly theorized as a corrective available to them if they would simply decide to use it.

However, her mature fiction is certainly more nuanced in its assessment of subjectivity among the oppressed. The aspirations, struggles, and negotiations of her heroines, in particular, Maggie Tulliver from *The Mill on the Floss* (1860) and Dorothea Brooke from *Middlemarch* (1872), are powerfully rendered, but it is perhaps Eliot's less heroic women who are more interesting in what they imply about the impact of social context on subjectivity and self-awareness. Eliot is very adept at revealing how an individual such as Rosamond Vincy from *Middlemarch* exists within a subjective experience of the world that is socially constructed and continuously reinforced. Trained in femininity at the finishing school of Mrs. Lemon and a product of both economic privilege and familial indulgence, she is self-satisfied, self-assured, and selfish, though certainly *not* self-centred in Fuller's sense of acquiring any intellectual and moral distance from contextual values. She is also incapable of seeing the world from the viewpoint of her fiancé and then husband, Lydgate, whose career aspirations are wholly foreign to her value system. Indeed, her worldview makes such complete and seamless sense to her that even though she endures significant setbacks and numerous frustrations, her conventionality inexorably overpowers Lydgate's somewhat less traditional vision of himself and his life with her. In the novel's closing paragraphs, we find that she "continued to be mild in her temper, inflexible in her judgment, disposed to admonish her husband, and able to frustrate him by stratagem. As the years went on he opposed her less and less, whence Rosamond concluded that he had learned the value of her opinion" (Eliot 1981a: 808). She, he claims, is "his basil plant . . . a plant which . . . flourished wonderfully on a murdered man's brains" (808). That sturdy, even vegetative existence – one steadily reinforced by social institutions and common values – is revealed to be difficult to oppose effectively or even to disrupt or complicate significantly. Indeed, such entrenchedness is why Eliot as a psychological realist never portrays in her novels anything other than incremental changes and small successes. She is a master at revealing the many, deep-seated impediments to critical self-awareness. As she says of another character from *Middlemarch* "Will not a tiny speck very close to our vision blot out the glory of the world and leave only a margin by which we see the blot? I know of no speck so troublesome as self" (407). The precise dynamic by which one not only sees past the blot but also gains some larger perspective on, and agency over, the blot is difficult to imagine for Eliot, as it is for other theorists of subjectivity.

It is worth noting that one, albeit highly unpleasant, avenue for change occasionally rendered in her novels is that of profound trauma, which can lead at times to altered selfhood and even nascent forms of self-awareness. Even the selfish and smug Tom Tulliver is subject to "a certain awe and humiliation" (Eliot 1981b: 545), as death approaches in the concluding paragraphs of *The Mill on the Floss*. Trauma is also the catalyst for growth and change in Gwendolyn Harleth in *Daniel Deronda* (1876). Through the harsh realities of economic deprivation and then a disastrous marriage to a man whose inflexible will exceeds her ability to manipulate or tactically counter, she is jolted out of the stasis of vain self-importance. After her husband's death and through interactions with the novel's eponymous hero, Gwendolyn comes to recognize that she "*was* selfish" in her earlier life (Eliot 1995: 766): "she was for the first time being dislodged from her supremacy in her own world, and getting a sense that her horizon was but a dipping onward of an existence with which her own was revolving" (804). Thus when we leave her at the end of the novel, Eliot gives us reason to believe Gwendolyn when she says to her mother "I shall live. I shall be better" (807). Throughout her writings, Eliot makes it clear that, she, unlike J. S. and Harriet Mill, demands significant self-awareness *before* full social enfranchisement, and for women trained in vanity, she seems to suggest that the only hope for even nascent self-awareness might be the sorts of profound crises and confrontations we see Gwendolyn experience. This hope that one can shock others into change may help us account for the harshness of Eliot's own rhetoric in lambasting "lady novelists," which actually anticipates that of the hectoring self-help gurus of the late twentieth century. She certainly highlights the particular problem of self-satisfaction *in* subjection, and how difficult it is to dislodge in any attempt to ameliorate, complicate, or tentatively politicize subjectivity. Indeed, how best to effect such consciousness-raising will be key to theories of class subjectivity as well as twentieth-century identity politics.

MARX, HEGEL, AND CLASS SUBJECTIVITY

John Stuart Mill's broad goal of extending to all the new freedom allowed by modern society, to make of oneself what one wishes, was the driving force behind most attempts to politicize selfhood during the nineteenth century. As noted earlier, this ideal of individuals rising in social standing as far as their desires, work habits, and talents would take them was unthinkable in earlier eras when an individual's station in life was considered fixed by nature and/or divine mandate. Yet key questions remained substantially unaddressed in liberal theory. If some individuals did not, or could not, rise, however hard they might work and however much they may desire to do so, was that failure still and always their own responsibility, or could it be attributable to the fundamental dynamics of a socio-economic system that could only function by keeping large numbers of individuals in disadvantaged circumstances? As Robbins notes above, liberal theory generally ignores many of the consequences and complexities of a competitive social ethos that by definition means there will be large numbers of losers as well as a few winners in the race for success. But during the era of Mill's writings, one major new theoretical perspective emerged that did begin to tackle those taken-for-granted inequities. Karl Marx (1818–83) provided some of the first and still some of the most incisive critiques of competitive capitalism, as he called for the revolutionary transformation of a naturalized economic system as well as the individual subjectivities that comprise it.

This is not to say that class consciousness originated with Marx. As I noted earlier, one of the watershed events signaling newly politicized subjectivities was the French Revolution of 1789, in which power was violently wrested from the corrupt and abusive French aristocracy. But the general mayhem and lack of sustained improvement in the lives of the masses in France after the revolution had several notable consequences. As Gary Day notes, "After the excesses of crowd behavior in the French Revolution, politicians were wary of trying to manipulate the 'mob,'" but even more importantly, the "French Revolution affected the development of the working class in two ways. First, it altered the language of political protest and, second, it made the authorities more repressive, thereby helping to create a sense of solidarity between different groups of workers" (Day 2001: 122–23). What was lacking until Marx, however, was a comprehensive theory of class exploitation and naturalized relations that could serve as a framework not only for effective critique, but also for precise action planning.

Yet Marx's theories also owed much to those of key philosophical predecessors, particularly the work of Georg Wilhelm Friedrich Hegel (1770–1831), whose rethinking of self-consciousness is important to note here. One of Hegel's most influential and enduring contributions to theories of subjectivity was his thorough historicizing of existence and self-conception. Peter Singer notes that Hegel advanced the idea that "the very foundations of the human condition could change from one historical era to another" (Singer 2001: 13), and he quotes Friedrich Engels, Marx's collaborator, who points to this "exceptional historical sense" (cit. Singer 2001: 13) as one of the keys to understanding Hegel's influence on Marxist theory. Moreover, beyond his general interest in the historical specificity of the human condition, Hegel was greatly concerned with demonstrating how the "history of the world is none other than the progress of the consciousness of freedom" (cit. Singer 2001: 15). While this appears to be compatible with the nineteenth-century liberal philosophical thought that we saw articulated by Mill, Hegel's theorization of the properties and particulars of self-consciousness, as it is impacted by this emerging consciousness of freedom, takes him in a dramatically different direction.

In Hegel's second section of his *Phenomenology of Spirit* (1806), entitled "Self-Consciousness," he makes the revolutionary claim that "Self-consciousness exists in and for itself when, and by the fact that, it so exists for another; that is, it exists only in being acknowledged" (Hegel 1977: 111). Hegel recognizes that an individual's self-consciousness never exists in isolation, that it always exists in relationship to an "other" or "others" who serve to validate its existence. But Hegel also suggests that this relationship is not one of inherent equality or mutual interpersonal validation; for Hegel, it always results in a struggle for domination: "Self-consciousness is faced by another self-consciousness; it has come *out of itself.* This has a twofold significance: first, it has lost itself, for it finds itself as an *other* being; secondly, in doing so it has superseded the other, for it does not see the other as an essential being, but in the other sees its own self. It must supersede this otherness of itself" (111). In fact, this uneasy dependence on the other leads to a form of "life-and-death" conflict (114) from which, finally, one of the two beings (or, as a broad social metaphor, *groups* of beings) emerges as a victor and establishes a temporary master/slave relationship with the dominated other. Yet as Singer notes, even "this situation is not stable" for though in conquering the other "it seems like the master has everything,"

Consider now the master's need for acknowledgement. He has the

> acknowledgement of the slave, to be sure, but in the eyes of the master the slave is merely a thing, not an independent consciousness at all. The master has, after all, failed to achieve the acknowledgement that he requires . . . Nor is the situation of the slave as it first appeared to be. The slave lacks adequate acknowledgement, of course, for to the master he is a mere thing. On the other hand, the slave works in the external world . . . [He] shapes and fashions the material objects on which he works. In doing so he makes his own ideas into something permanent, an external object . . . Through this process the slave becomes more aware of his own consciousness, for he sees it in front of him as something objective. In labour, even labour under the direction of another, hostile mind, the slave discovers that he has a mind of his own.
>
> (80–81)

This, in a nutshell, constitutes the Hegelian dialectical process at work on consciousness, as antagonistic forces in their inherent inadequacy come to clash and create through and beyond their conflict new syntheses, new forms and modes of being. It was this key point that Marx appropriated and augmented significantly, creating a theory of class consciousness and inevitable conflict that would dramatically expand the world's understanding of, and ability to, deploy the idea of politicized *group* subjectivity.

Marx thereby offers a major re-theorization of subjectivity, for he suggests that not only individual identity but also the human condition itself can change if formerly disconnected and apolitical individuals (Hegel's "slaves," broadly speaking) come together and recognize a shared experience of oppression and a common cause. Marx traces this process of radicalization and agency acquisition in his and Engels' "Manifesto of the Communist Party" (1848). Following Hegel's dialectical model, Marx and Engels first isolate what they believe has been a general move toward a distinct polarization of society "into two great hostile camps, into two great classes directly facing each other: Bourgeoisie and Proletariat" (Marx and Engels 1978: 474). Yet this self-interested antagonism is not immediately self-conscious; initially it is only a structural component and effect of capitalism. Downtrodden and disconnected laborers certainly will "struggle [at times] with the bourgeoisie," but "[a]t first the contest is carried on by individual laborers [only], then by the workpeople of a factory, then by the operatives of one trade, in one locality, against the individual bourgeois who directly exploits them" (480). Gradually, however, political self-consciousness begins to awaken, for "with the development of industry the proletariat not only increases in number; it becomes concentrated in greater masses, its strength grows, and it feels that strength more" (480). Disconnected, and relatively apolitical, *individual* identity is slowly subsumed into a powerful, politicized *group* identity: "This union is helped on by improved means of communication that are created by modern industry and that places the workers of different localities in contact with one another. It was just this contact that was needed to centralise the numerous local struggles, all of the same character into one national struggle between classes" (481). To be sure, this group consciousness, or self-aware union, is always fragile: "This organisation of the proletarians into a class, and consequently into a political party, is continually being upset again by the competition between the workers themselves. But it ever rises up again, stronger, firmer, mightier" (481). In line with the theories of Hegel, this process is tied inextricably to a growing and irreversible awareness of possibilities for greater freedom for greater numbers of people: "All previous historical movements are movements of minorities, or the interests of minorities. The proletarian movement is the self-conscious, independent movement of the immense majority" (482).

Yet even as Marx and Engels suggest that proletarian political self-consciousness is a historical inevitability, they also theorize a need for direct action in creating and sustaining it. In fact, the purpose of the "Manifesto" was one of actual consciousness-*raising*, of working to create that awareness of a common cause and agenda. Thus Marx and Engels assert that the "Communist Party" distinguishes itself from "other working-class parties by this only":

(1) In the national struggles of the proletarians of the different countries, they point out and bring to the front the common interests of the entire proletariat, independently of all nationality. (2) In the various stages of development which the struggle of the working class against the bourgeoisie has to pass through, they always and everywhere represent the interests of the movement as a whole.

> The Communists, therefore, are on the one hand, practically, the
> most advanced and resolute section of the working-class parties of
> every country, that section which pushes forward all others; on the other
> hand, theoretically, they have over the great mass of the proletariat the
> advantage of clearly understanding the line of march, the conditions,
> and the ultimate general results of the proletarian movement.
>
> (483–84)

Thus Communist Party members were charged with (or, more accurately, charge themselves with) working relentlessly to politicize the working class and to clarify for the proletariat generally how it was in their interest to shift their identity bases to a specific political group affiliation, one that takes precedence even over traditional national affiliation: "The working men have no country. . . . Since the proletariat must first of all acquire political supremacy, must rise to the leading class of the nation, must constitute itself *the* nation, it is, so far, itself national, though not in the bourgeois sense of the word" (488). Marx and Engels thereby issue one of the first explicit calls for self-aware decision-making in relation to one's identity, demanding a re-constitution of that identity through a self-conscious decision to place group political interests above all other possible affiliations, including formerly sacrosanct national ones.

Thus Marx and Engels, to an unprecedented degree, evacuate subjectivity of any essential or trans-historical quality, arguing instead that "man's ideas, views, and conceptions, in one word, man's consciousness, changes with every change in the conditions of his material existence, in his social relations and in his social life" (489). However, in suggesting that man also has the ability to change those same material conditions, they open up identity, theoretically at least, to an almost limitless degree of control. Charles Taylor therefore suggests that Marx is the clear "heir of the radical Enlightenment . . . in his notion that man comes to shape nature and eventually society to his purposes" (Taylor 1975: 547). "Under communism," Taylor says, "men freely shape and alter whatever social arrangements exist. They treat them as instruments" (552). Indeed, Marx argues in his "Preface" to *A Contribution to the Critique of Political Economy* (1859) that "It is not the consciousness of men that determines their existence, but their social existence that determines their consciousness," yet he also suggests clearly that a broad meta-consciousness is possible whereby men come to understand how such consciousness-determining "property relations" are in fact "fetters" (Marx 1970: 21). This inside/ outside movement of consciousness is, in fact, the process through which one gains a critical awareness of "ideology," of politically consequential, social belief that has been passed off as natural fact.

Indeed, the possibility that one can gain control over that which has controlled one's consciousness *by becoming conscious of that dynamic of control* is the premise of most twentieth-century theories of politicized subjectivity, though with a wide variety of relations being newly identified as fetters. The exposure of naturalized relations as fetters, the revelation of the *real* as in fact *ideological*, remains the mechanism by which most identity political movements even today theorize their own agency in promoting social change. Taylor notes that

> The idea of overcoming the injustice and expressive deadness of our world at one stroke by recovering control and radically reshaping it according to a freely chosen design exercises a profound attraction well beyond the boundaries of official Marxism. We find it almost everywhere among the protest and liberation movements of our day.
>
> (Taylor 1975: 539)

Thus Taylor makes the impressive point that all identity political movements today owe much to Marx and his predecessors' theories of instrumentality: "As transposed by Hegel and again by Marx, the Kantian aspiration to radical autonomy turns into the idea that human nature is not simply a given, but is to be made over. To be integrally free man must reshape his own nature" (Taylor 1975: 561).

Yet as empowering as this sounds, certainly instrumentality had and has its implicit theoretical limits. One is never theorized as completely free to assume whatever identity one wishes, to move freely across the lines of gender, race, or class. Indeed, a clear source of controversy raised by Marx, and one that will continue to concern later theorists, is the question of the extent to which *any* individual clearly outside of the newly politicized identity group – of workers, women, African-Americans, etc. – can have any role to play within or alongside the new political movement. Though Day rightly identifies "some ambiguity" on this issue in Marx (Day 2001: 128), Marx, more or less, implies that the inevitable antagonism of the proletariat and bourgeoisie makes it impossible for the latter to contribute to the cause of the former, especially given that the former must be committed to the wholesale destruction of the latter. Indeed, most dialectical thinking following Hegel was, and still remains, dependent upon such a dynamic of binary opposition and inevitable clash. This model of rigid polarization, and the political exclusion that it demands, may seem harsh and simplistic, but the underlying concern of its proponents always was, and is, with the establishment of an absolutely trustworthy political base that clearly and unequivocally represents the interests of the oppressed rather than serves covertly to reassert or justify the interests of the dominant group.

A glance at a key figure of British working-class literature of the nineteenth century lends some credence to this fear. In response to the Chartist movement, in which British workers of the 1830s–1850s agitated violently for expanded voting rights and better working conditions, the Reverend Charles Kingsley (1819–75) came to style himself a spokesperson for the interests of the oppressed. Though by birth and profession clearly a member of the middle class, Kingsley in 1849 even made the startling public announcement, "I am a Chartist" (cit. Chitty 1975: 123). But as I have argued elsewhere ("On the Making and Unmaking of Monsters" [Hall 1994]), Kingsley's "Christian socialism," as he termed it, was in fact an attempt to placate and manipulate the working class, and, finally, to keep them in their place. In his essays published under the pseudonym "Parson Lot" in the workingman's weekly *Politics for the People* Kingsley recommended to his working-class readers patience, sobriety, and above all "self"-mastery, with that last quality depending upon a conquering of all self-interest and, in fact, a renunciation of oppositional subjectivity: be content with "*the patient abiding of the meek*" rather than resort to the "frantic boasts of the bloodthirsty," he counsels (Kingsley *et al.* 1848: 136). Kingsley, not an oppressed worker himself, perceived working-class political self-interest as selfishness, a charge that will resurface time and again vis-à-vis later identity political movements as conservative interests ask the oppressed to give up their self-interested demands, to place the supposed "good" of society as a whole above their own search for political redress or justice. Thus Kingsley's novel *Alton Locke* (1850) delivers finally a very conservative social message couched in the form of seemingly progressive statements on improving the conditions of the working class; while sympathetic to the plight of other oppressed workers, Kingsley's working-class hero becomes thoroughly disenchanted with the organized labor movement and finally dedicates himself to a Christian philosophy of patience and humility (and dies peacefully soon thereafter). And the most telling aspect of Kingsley's participation in the social dialogue on Chartism is that by all indications, he *thought* he was being helpful and was serving as an ally of the oppressed (see my *Fixing Patriarchy* [1996a], Chapter 3, for a lengthier discussion).

For Marx, this blindness to the tendentiousness of one's own perspective is the result of thoroughly naturalized class relations and ideological programming. He says famously in his pamphlet *The Eighteenth Brumaire of Louis Bonaparte* (1852), "Men make their own history, but they do not make it just as they please. . . . The tradition of all the dead generations weighs like a nightmare on the brain of the living" (cit. Hawkes 1996: 92). He continues: "one must not form the narrow-minded opinion that the petty bourgeois, on principle, wishes to enforce an egoistic class interest. Rather, it believes that the *special* conditions of its emancipation are the *general* conditions within which alone modern society can be saved and the class struggle avoided" (cit. Hawkes 1996: 94). Thus intentions, good or ill, are not directly at issue here; instead Marx and later theorists are much more interested in that which we are programmed to believe and do. Clearly this programming, the processes by which it was effected, and its many consequences, were also of implicit interest to the commentators on race and gender mentioned earlier. But, most tellingly, it was appropriated as the domain of the new "social scientists" as the nineteenth century moved toward its close. And in particular it became the property of the new discipline of psychology, which assumed a position of objectivity in commenting on such programming, in effect, denying wholly its own political positioning even as it inevitably encoded, enforced, and reinforced certain identity political interests.

FREUD AND THE RISE OF THE SOCIAL SCIENCES

The Victorian era saw the creation and dramatic expansion of numerous new domains of theorization and knowledge creation. While previously, and as we have explored thus far, investigations of human existence and society were integral to the discipline of philosophy, the nineteenth century was one of subdivision and proliferating specialization in the natural sciences and, most tellingly, the new social sciences. Thus the French sociologist Émile Durkheim (1858–1917) in his *The Division of Labor in Society* (1893) asserts that specialization is the most significant social change distinguishing his century from previous ones: "in higher societies our duty lies not in extending the range of our activity but in concentrating it, in making it more specialised. We must limit our horizons, select a definite task, and involve ourselves utterly. . . . [T]his specialization must be carried the farther the more society is of a higher species" (Durkheim 1984: 333). Furthermore, he connects this duty to specialize one's activities with the spread of personal individualization in so-called "higher" societies, where "psychological life of a new kind makes its appearance. . . . Individual personalities are formed and become conscious of themselves" (285).

Yet as chaotic as all of this self-interested activity sounds, Durkheim also implies that someone or something still needs to direct it; he notes, "The new life that all of a sudden has arisen has not been able to organize itself thoroughly. Above all, it has not been organized so as to satisfy the need for justice that has been aroused even more passionately in our hearts" (339). Throughout *The Rules of Sociological Method* (1895) he implies that the field of sociology occupies that particularly crucial, *organizational* and *instrumental*, role in the new array of discretely defined disciplines and individualities; near the end of the book, he sums up:

> We have shown how the sociologist had to lay aside the preconceived notions that he held about the facts in order to confront the facts themselves; how he had to penetrate to them through their most objective characteristics; how he had to address himself to them in order to find a means of classifying them as healthy or pathological.
>
> (Durkheim 1982: 161)

Of course, religion formerly addressed itself to that work of distinguishing healthy from pathological activity. As Beryl Langer notes, Durkheim "believed that the problems generated by the collapse of traditional order would only be solved on the basis of scientific understanding of how societies worked. If the laws governing the natural world could be discovered through empirical observation, so too could the laws of the social world" (Langer 1991: 70).

It is important to note that this emphasis on the dramatic new insights allowed by a supposed "objective" study of human behavior was actually initiated much earlier in the century by another French thinker, Auguste Comte (1798–1857) who, in his six-volume set of lectures *The Positive Philosophy* (1830–42), can be credited with coining the phrase "sociology," the culminating discipline that, in his opinion, offers final answers to questions of human being and interaction. In his *System of Positive Polity* (1851–54) he goes so far as to suggest that *all* rules of human behavior and social organization are open to wholly rational decision-making. As Thomas Leahey notes, Comte believed that with "the ability to predict nature comes the ability to control nature. Hence, when a science of humanity emerges, society and individuals will likewise be subject to control" (Leahey 1987: 145).

Yet as much as this line of sociological thought running directly from Comte to Durkheim would seem to suggest an unflappable faith in objective social description and prescription, the understanding of human behavior was/is hardly reducible to the discovery of a system of broad rules and a quasi-scientific perfection of processes of rational thinking. In Germany, such inescapable human variability and unpredictability led to the birth of Wilhelm Wundt's (1832–1920) "psychology of consciousness," which Leahey accurately points to as the progenitor of today's scientific psychology, and in particular, Wundt's use of controlled experiments that probed variations in perception, attention span, and retention (Leahey 1987: 179–88). Similarly, the British social scientist Herbert Spencer (1820–1903), in his application of Darwinian theories to sociology and individual psychology, was interested not only in large social patterns but also individual manifestations of adaptation. In fact, Spencer produced theories that were so invested in processes of adaptation that they were quite draconian in their indifference to those people(s) who lost an imagined grand struggle for the survival of the fittest, and that were unabashedly racist in their designation of advanced and inferior categories of human beings.

However, it was Sigmund Freud (1856–1939) and his psychology of the unconscious that most clearly contested any blind faith in rational control over human behavior and social life, though he too participates in the broad search for a reliable social scientific methodology described above. As Charles Taylor notes, "Freud takes a Cartesian stance to [the] inner world. The aim is by objectifying it to gain a disengaged understanding of it and, as a consequence, to liberate us from its obsessions, terrors, compulsions" (Taylor 1989: 446). Indeed, Freud's theory of therapeutic intervention can be interpreted as one of the most powerful manifestations of a general desire for instrumental control over subjectivity and the intense interest during this era in normalizing those self-identities perceived as socially aberrant or improperly restrained. As Freud himself states, "psychoanalysis . . . was originally the name of a particular therapeutic method, [but] it has now become the name of a science, the science of unconscious mental processes" (Freud 1957b: 37).

Freud's major contributions to the ongoing discussion of subjectivity were a revolutionary emphasis on the developmental aspects of individual psychology and a recognition of the powerful influence of the unconscious on conscious life. As Pamela Thurschwell suggests, Freudian psychoanalysis "provides both a theory of the history of the individual mind – its early development, its frustrations and desires (which include sexual, or what Freud calls libidinal, desires) – and a set of specific therapeutic techniques for recalling, interpreting, and coming to terms with that individual history" (Thurschwell 2000: 2). In his *Three Essays on the Theory of Sexuality* (1905) and other works, Freud suggested that adult human consciousness and identity is the culmination of a complicated childhood developmental process that includes various crises, with often unsteady resolutions. While countless books have been published detailing the intricacies of Freudian theory, it is most important to note here that Freud uniquely isolated familial context and erotic/sexual desire as integral to the development of adult identity. As the child moves through various stages in her/his early life, corresponding roughly to a gratification of desires associated with various bodily regions (oral, anal, and genital), frustrations and rivalries occur inevitably within the nuclear family, ones that necessitate a sublimation and redirection of desires into socially acceptable channels. The unconscious is the repository of the excess that is inexorably and necessarily excluded from what is deemed "normal" adult social existence. As Thurschwell defines it,

[the] unconscious . . . is primarily the storehouse of instinctual desires and needs. Childhood wishes and memories live on in unconscious life, even if they have been erased from consciousness. The unconscious life is, in a sense, the great waste-paper basket of the mind – the trash that never gets taken out.

(4)

In his "A Note on the Unconscious in Psychoanalysis" (1912), Freud specifies that the "term unconscious . . . designates not only latent ideas in general, but especially ideas with a certain dynamic character" (Freud 1957c: 49). He elaborates in *Civilization and Its Discontents* (1930): "in mental life nothing which has once been formed can perish – . . . everything is somehow preserved and . . . in suitable circumstances . . . it can once more be brought to light" (cit. Thurschwell 2000: 4).

Freudian theory is at once descriptive and prescriptive, or in Freud's words above, "scientific" and "therapeutic." As Anthony Easthope notes, Freud the social scientist constructs a "map or model of the psychic apparatus, his 'topography' . . . [and] gave priority to three different agencies, ego, id and super-ego" with the ego representing conscious life, the id forming the "reservoir of libido or psychic energy" and the super-ego functioning as "the voice of conscience and censorship" (Easthope 1999: 44). Yet description was never psychology's sole purpose. In *Beyond the Pleasure Principle* (1920), Freud traces a burgeoning interventionist role for the psychoanalyst:

Five-and-twenty years have brought about a complete change in the more immediate aims of psychoanalytic work. At first the endeavors of the analytic physician were confined to divining the unconscious of which his patient was unaware, effecting a synthesis of its various components and communicating it at the right time. Psychoanalysis was above all an art of interpretation.

(Freud 1957a: 148)

As this passage continues, however, both the tactic and Freud's actual verb change: "the next aim was to *compel* the patient . . . teaching him to abandon [his] resistances" (148–49, my emphasis). Immediately thereafter, Freud's verb alters yet again, taking its final and definitive form:

the "physician [now] makes it his concern . . . to *force* into memory as much as possible, and to leave as little as possible to repetition" (149, my emphasis).

Thus there are contradictory implications throughout Freud. One is that we are always at the mercy of forces, drives, and desires that are beyond our control, hidden away within that great storehouse of memories and forgotten experiences. Our subjectivity, our knowledge of individual selfhood and our degree of agency over that selfhood, is thereby more limited in Freudian theory than in that of any of the predecessors whom we considered earlier. However, Freudian theory does offer *itself* as a reliable map of human psychology that suggests a degree of influence, even if never absolute control, over subjectivity, if not for the individual subject, then certainly for the trained psychoanalyst interacting with the subject. Of course, unlike the theories of race, gender, and class covered earlier, Freudian notions of subjectivity do not imply agency through political or group self-awareness, but rather agency through the consultation of, and direction by, an authority figure. In fact, broadly speaking, psychoanalytic theory in its early Freudian manifestations comes into inevitable conflict with most theories of politicized subjectivity because to the extent that it implies agency, it is fundamentally a theory of agency in the pursuit of social normalization rather than one of agency in the urgent contestation of any unjust social values. The agency offered by Freudian theory is, most often, that of fostering and finding less anguished or conflicted conformity.

This is not, however, to dismiss the extraordinary insight into subjectivity offered by Freud. Individual and social life is always a series of negotiations between personal or micro-group desires and broad communal needs. Yet certainly the legacy of Freud is a complicated one. To recognize that our personalities, self-conceptions, and interactions with others are always haunted by the past is a powerful tool that enables us to better understand subjectivity. And Freud, especially late in life, had little real faith in therapy actually repairing aberrant personalities: "Our impression is that we must not be surprised if the difference between a person who has not and a person who has been analysed is, after all, not so radical as we endeavour to make it and expect and assert that it will be" (cit. Frosh 1999: 68). Despite this proviso, the emphasis remains on that strenuous *attempt* to alter the analysand, to bring her or him to a point of better integration into pre-existing social values and norms. While later theorists and interlocutors will revise Freud considerably (as we will see in our discussion of Lacan and Butler), late nineteenth/early twentieth-century psychoanalytic theory was only political in the sense of potentially allowing certain forms of broad cultural analysis; as Stephen Frosh notes, it "provides some criteria for the assessment of the relative worth of current social relations and of alternative social configurations" (Frosh 1999: 253). Thus as part of the constellation of social sciences that arose during that era, psychoanalysis sought to "discipline" subjectivity, both in the sense of making it a topic of intense study and making it conform to certain historically specific norms and ideals.

These aspects of the new field of psychology and psychoanalysis are useful in discussing literature around the turn of the century. The revelatory potential of psychology, especially in its emphasis on the hidden dynamics of human behavior and the limited possibilities for any instrumental control over our selves, is memorably explored in T. S. Eliot's poem "The Love Song of J. Alfred Prufrock" (1915). Eliot's narrator is fully aware of his tendency to procrastinate, his "hundred indecisions . . . hundred visions and revisions," but he remains paralyzed nevertheless. Prufrock attempts to work himself up to action, to press his case with the woman he desires, but he cannot, obsessing instead on scenarios of rejection. Indeed, Prufrock, in contradistinction to some social scientists' faith in rationality, demonstrates clearly the mundane limits of agency in any attempt to change one's selfhood. He is remarkably self-conscious and certainly aware of himself as a being that exists without natural or divine determinants, but he derives no agency from that state of awareness. Instead he is immobilized ("pinned and wriggling") by that very state of consciousness, and specifically, by being an object of possibly critical social scrutiny ("They will say: 'How his hair is growing thin!'" . . . "And I have known the eyes already, known them all – /The eyes that fix you in a formulated phrase"). As Peter Childs argues in *Modernism*, "Prufrock appears as a split being, another instance of the fragmented Modernist self split off from society, caught in language, neuroses and psychological self-doubts" (Childs 2000: 102). Writing in the era of the birth of psychology, Eliot demonstrates the extraordinary richness of the terrain of the inner life. Nothing overt happens in the poem, yet a compelling psychological struggle is certainly portrayed for the reader.

The poem explores stasis and lack of self-directed agency, but in a broader sense it does *do* something, which leads us to the other implication of psychology as a new and powerful discipline. Childs argues that Eliot demonstrates the extent to which "the poet and poetry itself became in many ways etherized: antihumanist, undermined by hidden desires, driven by the unconscious, lost in language, painfully self-conscious, apolitical and detached" (102). However, I would suggest a very different reading, that in foregrounding precisely those aspects of modern life, the poet most certainly is *not* trapped in Prufrock's own state of paralysis, and nor does he imply that we should be. The psychological limit-case of Prufrock is clearly designed to startle and to instruct. Its revelation of the sterility of the lives of the upper classes ("In the room the women come and go/Talking of Michelangelo") is certainly critical, even broadly political in implication, as Frosh might point out. And if we see ourselves, or aspects of ourselves, in Eliot's narrator, the consequence is not one of celebrating or validating our own indecisions. As a psychological case study in social and, arguably, sexual impotence, "The Love Song of J. Alfred Prufrock" may affirm our lack of instrumentality, but also presses us to avoid drowning in the sea of our own anxieties as its narrator does in the poem's last phrase. It attempts to shock us into action, to seek help, possibly even to enter therapy, since it demonstrates clearly that our ability to think ourselves out of our own neuroses is highly limited, even doomed to failure.

Such psychological explorations often serve as opportunities for subtle social commentary and sophisticated probing of the limits of agency in our lives. But even so, authority-driven therapy and other supposed cures for psychological afflictions came in for increasing condemnation in literature around the turn of the century. While specifically Freudian psychotherapy was not the direct target of works such as Charlotte Perkins Gilman's "The Yellow Wall-Paper" (1890) and Virginia Woolf's *Mrs. Dalloway* (1925), those texts decry the growing investment of social power in medical professionals, who are authorized to intervene unilaterally in the lives of those deemed aberrant or psychologically disordered. In Woolf's novel, this is explored in the disastrous treatment of Septimus Warren Smith, whose shell shock after returning from the Great War is so insensitively handled that he finally kills himself rather than submit to the direction of Dr. William Bradshaw and others. Indeed, Woolf demonstrates that when the newly empowered psychological establishment asserts its absolute, self-confident authority over a so-called "case," no subjective agency is granted to the patient him/herself. Smith's words, desires, and expressed needs are wholly dismissed; he is simply "sick" and is told he must submit to the doctor's prescription. "'Must,' 'must,' why 'must'?" he thinks, before he flings "himself vigorously, violently down on to Mrs. Filmer's area railings" (Woolf 1981: 146–48). Self-destruction is the only power he possesses over his self.

Similarly, Gilman's narrator, suffering from a supposed "temporary nervous depression" (Gilman 1995: 3), is literally incarcerated in the nursery of her own home, forbidden to write or work, and driven slowly mad by the very rest cure imposed by her doctor/husband. While he cautions her to exercise "proper self-control" (4), in fact, she is allowed no agency at all, and is, like Septimus, required to submit fully to her husband's (the doctor's) authority over her "case" (5). Granted, she does find a limited mode of self-expression in her increasingly aberrant activities (see Hall 2003: 122–23), yet certainly her story is constructed primarily as a shocking, cautionary tale concerning the hidden agenda of the contemporary medical/psychological establishment: the enforcement of rigid gender roles, the glorification of medical authority at the expense of the patient, and the wholesale denial of individual needs and subject positions through the imposition of an inflexible psychological template onto those perceived as ill or aberrant. The narrator's subjectivity is, of course, the topic of the story but is of no interest to her physician husband, whose only desire is to inculcate obedience and conformity. Gilman's and Woolf's narratives reveal that in this era of burgeoning interest in psychology and a new recognition of flexibility in social self-creation, one clear consequence was the eager investment by social scientists in new rules and mechanisms for normalization, even as politicized selfhood also meant a growing interest in challenging highly tendentious definitions of normality. This is one of the major conflicts that will manifest itself variously over succeeding decades and that later sections of this book will examine.

Yet the broad field of psychology always encompassed more than simply rigid and authoritative diagnoses by empowered medical personnel. One other manifestation of a continuing interest and investment in personal agency in the nineteenth century is worth mentioning here, for it has become a widespread cultural phenomenon in the twentieth century. The year 1859 saw the publication of Samuel Smiles's *Self-Help*; as Walter Houghton notes in *The Victorian Frame of Mind*, "20,000 young men in the year of publication . . . and 130,000 more in the next thirty years bought [it]" (Houghton 1957: 191), with, of course, countless others consulting it through lending libraries. The book developed out of a series of lectures delivered to working-class men by the author, and is presented primarily in the form of case studies of successful men, their work habits and attitudes. First and foremost, it offers itself unabashedly as a program for acquiring those masculine identity traits that makes one successful in meeting the needs of an economically and imperially expanding nation; it extols perseverance, energy, and courage among other manly attributes, and links them all, tellingly, with the supposed inherent makeup of the "Teutonic race" in its seventh chapter. Thus it is important to note that "self-help" here and in its popular twentieth/twenty-first century manifestations inevitably transmits cultural beliefs regarding such categories as gender, race, and class. And in arguing "the best institutions can give a man no active aid. Perhaps the utmost they can do is, to leave him *free* to develop himself and improve his individual condition" (Smiles: 15), Smiles is clearly complicit with conservative, *laissez-faire* political interests that would minimize or eliminate the role of government in ensuring or even attending to the general social welfare. The individual is perceived as an autonomous unit who is solely responsible for his or her own success or failure.

Yet equally noteworthy is that Smiles ascribes an extraordinary amount of agency to the individual: "It may be of comparatively little consequence how a man is governed from without, whilst everything depends upon how he governs himself from within" (17). This is the theory of instrumental selfhood at its most seductive and still today most widely embraced. It drew upon and popularized Romantic notions of individualism and self-sufficiency, ones that also animated the work of American Transcendentalists, including Margaret Fuller, whom we discussed earlier, Ralph Waldo Emerson (1803–82), and Henry David Thoreau (1817–62). And indeed, it is important to remember that the self-help movement, while often mouthing simple-minded formulae for achieving greater social conformity and narrowly defined forms of success, became so popular in the twentieth century because it offered a private and personal alternative to the more rigid and authority-driven one-on-one therapy industry. While hardly liberating, it was a mechanism for individualistic interpretation and manipulation of general psychological insights without having to answer to or report results to anyone else. Of course, this experience of autonomy has numerous consequences. As men and, for some writers, women too were theorized as increasingly free to make of themselves whatever they desired, the anxieties over what to do with that freedom also became ever more intense.

NIETZSCHE AND THE EXISTENTIALISTS

How best to live in this state of *potential* freedom became the singular concern of existentialist philosophers, from Nietzsche through Sartre, Camus, and others. Even as psychologists of the late nineteenth and early twentieth centuries began to focus on the weighty influence of the unconscious on our daily lives, the existentialists asserted the necessity of making one's life as fully conscious as possible, whatever limitations one might inevitably encounter: "What matters – all that matters, really – is the will to happiness, a kind of enormous, ever-present consciousness" (Camus 1972: 128). It was not that existentialists dismissed outright all of the insights of the social sciences, but they certainly were suspicious of the determinist implications of theories of social and psychological conditioning, which they feared were simply another set of rigid constraints replacing those of religion and traditional belief: "Empirical psychoanalysis . . . is based on the hypothesis of the existence of an unconscious psyche, which on principle escapes the intuition of the subject. Existential psychoanalysis rejects the hypothesis of the unconscious" (Sartre 1992: 728). As Neil Levy notes, for the existentialists, "there are no drives, no barriers, and certainly no divisions within [consciousness]" (Levy 2002: 82). Instead, existentialists explored the necessity of always working consciously and honestly on one's selfhood: "Of all the men he had carried inside himself, as every man does at the beginning of this life, of all those various rootless, mingling beings, he had created his life with consciousness, with courage. That was his whole happiness in living and dying" (Camus 1972: 147). Indeed, forthrightly "contemplating [man's] freedom" (Camus 1972: 73), scorning those who "feared and exalted impotence" (Camus 1972: 147), calling "cowards" those who "hide from . . . freedom, in the guise of solemnity or with deterministic excuses" (Sartre 1975: 366) was the existentialist response to both lingering, tradition-based and new, quasi-scientific thought barriers to the continuing ideal of instrumentally controlled selfhood.

This unabashedly post-Christian idealization of instrumentality began with Friedrich Nietzsche (1844–1900). Of course, as iconoclastic as Nietzsche was, his was a voice that added to an ongoing conversation about possible bases for forthright personal action and responsible social interaction in a context in which traditional belief systems were being undermined and discredited. As early as the mid-nineteenth century, the forefather of existentialism, Søren Kierkegaard (1813–55), began to assert the necessity of embracing creativity and individualism, especially in one's relationship to God, about whose very existence Kierkegaard seems highly anxious. The theories of Charles Darwin (1809–82) and the rise of science as the primary means by which the past, present, and future of human existence could be understood are key developments here. Yet Darwin's theories and their translation into social science by Herbert Spencer and others were not only threatening to religious thinkers, they posed challenges to all philosophers who based their theories in the possibility of confident self-aware action-planning. As Peter Childs notes, "All of these thinkers [e.g. Darwin, Spencer], while offering liberating ideas of human change and progress, also proposed theories which overwhelmed individual agency or will within new systems of vast collective social and biological forces" (Childs 2000: 37).

Indeed, that is one reason why Nietzsche distanced himself from Darwinian thought, for though he certainly respected Darwin's challenge to traditional religious beliefs, Nietzsche's philosophy was one that celebrated the activity of creative and self-empowered individuals in this new post-religious context. Thus in his posthumously published notes entitled *The Will to Power* (1901), we find an entry from *c.*1883–88 in which he asserts, "The influence of 'external circumstances' is overestimated by Darwin to a ridiculous extent: the essential thing in the life process is precisely the tremendous shaping, form-creating force working from within which *utilizes* and *exploits* 'external circumstances'" (Nietzsche

1968: 344). And tellingly, in an entry dated 1888, Nietzsche dismisses a key Darwinian assertion, maintaining instead that "man as a species is not progressing. Higher types are indeed attained, but they do not last. The level of the species is *not* raised" (Nietzsche 1968: 363). Since Nietzsche believes that a ubiquitous "herd-like" timidity and conformity tend to overwhelm those rare individuals who are unique and forward-thinking, he argues, "Strange though it may sound, one always has to defend the strong against the weak; the fortunate against the unfortunate; the healthy against those degenerating and afflicted with hereditary traits" (Nietzsche 1968: 364).

Certainly we should not rely too heavily for our argument here on the private and disconnected notes arranged into *The Will to Power* by Nietzsche's fascistically inclined sister Elisabeth. But Alexander Nehamas, who references that text generously, does make a very compelling argument in his *Nietzsche: Life as Literature* that Nietzsche advocated a willful shaping of one's life into an aesthetic product that gives it meaning and importance.

> The self, according to Nietzsche, is not a constant, stable entity. On the contrary, it is something one becomes, something, he would even say, one constructs. . . . [A] person worthy of admiration, a person who has (or is) a self, is one whose thoughts, desires, and actions are not haphazard but are instead connected to one another in the intimate way that indicates in all cases the presence of style. A self is just a set of coherently connected episodes. . . . Coherence, of course, can also be produced by weakness, mediocrity, and one-dimensionality. But style, which is what Nietzsche requires and admires, involves controlled multiplicity and resolved conflict.
>
> (Nehamas 1985: 7)

Into the potentially meaningless void of post-traditional society, Nietzsche introduces the idea of a chosen, willful meaning creation that may not be possible for all in his view, but certainly for the honest, brave, and intellectually strong.

This sounds quite elitist, and Nietzsche does often express scorn for the timid, herd-like masses. Yet even in the act of writing and publishing his ideas, Nietzsche seems to suggest that his theories can have an effect on his audience, potentially even a wide and profound one. He writes in his autobiography *Ecce Homo* (published posthumously in 1908), "The last thing *I* should promise would be to 'improve' mankind. No new idols are erected by me. . . . *Overthrowing idols* (my word for 'ideals') – that comes closer to being part of my craft" (Nietzsche 1969: 217–18). However, he certainly does not underestimate the effect of such iconoclasm; in the same text he writes, "I know my fate. One day my name will be associated with the memory of something tremendous – a crisis without equal on earth, the most profound collision of conscience, a decision that was conjured up *against* everything that had been believed, demanded, hallowed so far. I am no man, I am dynamite" (326). And he was not far off the mark, for Nietzsche certainly has been widely referenced, used, and misused as the spokesperson for a new era: post-Christian, free, and potentially frightening in its lack of a fixed moral base. Thus he asserts famously (or infamously, depending on one's point of view) in *The Gay Science* (1882), "After Buddha was dead, his shadow was still shown for centuries in a cave – a tremendous, gruesome shadow. God is dead; but given the way of men, there may still be caves for thousands of years in which his shadow will be shown. – And we – we still have to vanquish his shadow too" (Nietzsche 1974: 167).

This call to action, this implication of a common mission connecting him to his audience, is not as narrowly pitched as some commentators have maintained. It is a provocation and also an open invitation. In *The Gay Science* he answers the question "Who is most influential?" with "When a human being resists his whole age and stops it at the gate to demand an accounting, this *must* have influence" (198). "Influence" in this passage seems to indicate an effective proselytizing role. In *The Gay Science* and through his spokesperson/prophet Zarathustra in *Thus Spoke Zarathustra* (1883–92), Nietzsche engages in a process of forthright consciousness raising that is clearly intended to inculcate a greater degree of personal agency and the taking of responsibility for one's action in the process of self-creation, and that is hardly limited to the rare exception or some imagined future *Ubermensch*. He seeks to empower generally when he writes in *The Gay Science*:

> For believe me: the secret for harvesting from existence the greatest fruitfulness and the greatest enjoyment is – to *live dangerously*. Build

your cities on the slopes of Vesuvius! Send your ships into uncharted seas! Live at war with your peers and yourselves! Be robbers and conquerors as long as you cannot be rulers and possessors, you seekers of knowledge! Soon the age will be past when you could be content to live hidden in forests like shy deer. At long last the search for knowledge will reach out for its due; it will want to *rule* and *possess*, and you with it!

(228–29)

Indeed, Nietzsche's is yet another nineteenth-century manifestation of a quasi-self-help philosophy: "What is the history of every day in your case? Look at your habits that constitute it: are they the product of innumerable little cowardices and laziness or of your courage and inventive reason" (Nietzsche 1974: 246). This implies an unprecedented form of instrumental agency that replaces a divinely created nature with a new awareness of one's own socially and potentially self-constructed identity. And, indeed, it is that inside/outside move, from being passively constructed to being active in one's own construction of self, that remains fundamental to twentieth-century theories of personal and political empowerment through heightened critical consciousness. Nietzsche is the precursor of both the high theorists and the pop psychologists of the twentieth century who begin from the assumption that post-traditional, post-modern human beings have the historically unparalleled potential to "create themselves" (Nietzsche 1974: 266) if they simply have the will to do so.

As indicated above, that challenge to create new forms of selfhood, as one bravely faces the "death" of religion and other traditional belief systems, was taken up in the early to mid-twentieth century by the self-styled "existentialists." Jean-Paul Sartre (1905–80) notes in his key lecture/essay "Existentialism is a Humanism" (1946), that philosophical movement is perhaps best understood as a "meta-theory" of self-responsibility.

[T]here is no human nature, because there is no God to have a conception of it. Man simply is. Not that he is simply what he conceives himself to be, but he is what he wills, and as he conceives himself after already existing. . . . Man is nothing else but that which he makes of himself. That is the first principle of existentialism. And this is what people call its "subjectivity," using the word as a reproach against us. . . . Man is, indeed, a project which possesses a subjective life, instead of being a kind of moss, or a fungus or a cauliflower. . . . If, however, it is true that existence is prior to essence, man is responsible for what he is. Thus, the first effect of existentialism is that it puts every man in possession of himself as he is, and places the entire responsibility for his existence squarely upon his own shoulders.

(Sartre 1975: 349–50)

Sartre here takes basic Nietzschean insights and translates them into a direct challenge to his own audience and era: deal forthrightly with your existential aloneness and your self-responsibility. And the latter receives particular attention. The most common charge leveled against Nietzsche, Sartre, and others was, and still is, that they offer a vision of the world in which a common ethics is replaced with wholesale self-serving, solipsistic power-seeking. Indeed, Alexander Nehamas admits that there are no solid internal checks within Nietzsche's philosophy that would preclude the "objectionable, obnoxious, and even dangerous. . . . [H]is advice can be followed to the letter and result not simply in a mediocrity but in an actual monstrosity" (233).

Sartre, sensitive to this, addresses the issue explicitly:

And, when we say that man is responsible for himself, we do not mean that he is responsible only for his own individuality, but that he is responsible for all men. The word "subjectivism" is to be understood in two senses, and our adversaries play upon only one of them. Subjectivism means, on the one hand, the freedom of the individual subject and, on the other, that man cannot pass beyond human subjectivity. It is the latter which is the deeper meaning of existentialism. When we say that man chooses himself, we do mean that every one of us must choose himself; but by that we also mean that in choosing for himself he chooses for all men. For in effect, of all the actions a man may take in order to create himself as he wills to be, there is not one which is not creative, at the same time, of an image of man such as he believes he ought to be.

(Sartre 1975: 350)

As Sartre goes on to explain later in the same essay, this is not a new manifestation of the Kantian categorical imperative, for there are far too many nuanced situations that cannot be reduced to one simple rule governing everyone's behavior; Sartre's perspective and examples are much more supple and demanding of creative response than that. But certainly his worldview is one of grappling with ethics in self-creation rather than cleverly avoiding the entire topic. For as much as existentialism "has been reproached as an invitation to people to dwell in the quietism of despair" (Sartre 1975: 345), certainly Sartre's own political activism and energetic admonishments, in print and in public work, derive from his unwavering belief in *social* responsibility always attending individual freedom. He concludes with, "There is no other universe except the human universe, the universe of human subjectivity" and in the face of that maintains firmly that "existentialism is optimistic" (Sartre 1975: 368–69), for it implies an enormous creative and intellectual freedom in and scope for daily life.

This struggle between individual freedom and social responsibility in self-creation animates much of the literature of the first half of the twentieth century. It is a thematic climate that is signaled memorably in William Butler Yeats's "The Second Coming" from 1920. Like Woolf's *Mrs. Dalloway*, the poem conveys the shock and horror of the era around the Great War with its unparalleled carnage and senseless mass destruction. But it is not "Mere anarchy" (line 4) that the poem locates as its most profound concern. In its evocation of the image of "A shape with lion body and the head of a man" (line 14) whose hour has "come round at last" (line 21), the poem suggests that a new era of thinking brutality is upon us. Its "Second Coming" is the inauguration of a decidedly post-Christian era, in which "The best lack all conviction, while the worst/Are full of passionate intensity" (lines 7–8). The poem suggests clearly in its imagery of circularity and its diction ("The darkness drops *again*" in line 18, my emphasis) that this is a return, of a sort, to a pagan ethos. But its broader anxiety is over a new and far worse manifestation of a "world spirit," that is captured in its memorable image of the slouching, thinking "rough beast" (line 21), whose "blank and pitiless" gaze (line 15) signals the worst possible manifestation of a Nietzschean "will to power," from which all sympathy has been drained and replaced by a coupling of cunning and conscience-less strength. Of course, in offering this diagnosis or "revelation" the poem is hardly complicit with or resigned to this ethos; it asks its reader, in its open-ended final question ("what rough beast . . . Slouches towards Bethlehem to be born?") and through its clear desire to shock, to make a decision, take a stand, find a sense of empowerment and agency in opposing the tide of the time.

In glancing at other poems and novels of the era, one could find innumerable examples of individual characters choosing monstrously or responsibly in their capacities to create their own lives without the traditional constraints of religion or belief in fixed social place or role. Certainly Joseph Conrad's *Heart of Darkness* (1902) struggles with the implications of a quasi-Nietzschean philosophy of "freedom" in the character of Kurtz, who creates himself and who exercises an extraordinary amount of personal strength and power in his jungle enclave. Yet even if the narrator Marlowe (and the tale itself) is ambivalent in a conjoined respect for and horror over Kurtz's brazen, egotistical creativity, the novella finally shows just how self-destructive and horrible Kurtz's activities are, and evokes a far different ethos in its frame narrative of the Buddha-like Marlowe and in its broad condemnation of European greed, corruption, and self-willed ignorance. Here as in "The Second Coming," the point of the text is that something *else* is possible, that however irrevocable the breakdown of traditional beliefs may be, it is incumbent for the modern "subject" to create a new selfhood that is at once ethically engaged and strong enough to resist the pull of anarchy or the lure of easy wealth through colonial exploitation.

While much of the literature of the first half of the century was clearly cautionary given new possibilities for grotesquely immoral and destructive personae who create themselves in an ethical void, the existentialist philosophers mentioned above were certainly more interested in probing possible gray areas and nuances of the process of taking responsibility for the self in a post-traditional era. Any number of existentialist novels or plays would lend themselves to our discussion here, including André Gide's *The Immoralist* (1902), Jean Genet's *Our Lady of the Flowers* (1944), and Sartre's "No Exit" (1944), but one work stands out for its interest in the possibility of personal agency in the construction of a meaningful, even "happy" existence. Camus's *A Happy Death* was written between 1936 and 1938, but remained unpublished until 1971 (with an English translation following in 1972). Formally there are numerous problems with the novel that Camus never resolved before turning his full attention to writing *The Stranger* in 1939. But thematically, it is an extraordinary expression of the existentialist philosophy of consciously *making meaning* in the face of possibly paralyzing meaninglessness.

Its protagonist, Patrice Mersault, whom Camus reworked as the central character in *The Stranger*, is a man whose life in the novel's first section is a great blank of tedious work and shallow routine. But a chance meeting and then friendship with a physically disabled, wealthy, and self-destructive man, Zagreus, and an encounter with another individual, Cardona, whose life of appalling squalor and self-loathing seems to prefigure Mersault's own future, lead to a momentous change. Mersault kills Zagreus, with the latter's complicity and suicide note already supplied, and takes his money to embark on an experiment in actively creating a happy existence. The murder serves as a plot device, rather than an existentialist prescription or justification for violence, as it allows the novel to make a connection between an escape from poverty and the *possibility* of happiness; "you can't be happy without money" (Camus 1972: 43), Zagreus comments, as their conversations lay the philosophical groundwork for the murder/suicide. With the money and after some mistakes, Mersault does achieve happiness, briefly and memorably, as he lives the Nietzschean injunction to create one's life with a sense of aesthetic attachment: "Like any work of art, life needs to be thought through. Mersault thought about his life and exercised his bewildered consciousness and his longing for happiness" (74). He comes to the realization that "He had to create his happiness and his justification" (81); "To lick his life like barley sugar, to shape it, sharpen it, love it at last – that was his whole passion" (83). While never overtly acknowledging Nietzsche, the novel takes his concept of the "will to power" and rewrites it explicitly as the "will to happiness":

> What matters – all that matters, really – is the will to happiness, a kind of enormous, ever-present consciousness. The rest – women, art, success – is nothing but excuses. A canvas waiting for our embroideries. . . . You know the famous formula – "If I had my life to live over again" – well, I would live it over again just the way it has been.
>
> (128–29)

That is, in fact, the final Nietszchean test, of eternal recurrence, in which one must contemplate, construct, and come to accept one's life as an aesthetic creation worthy of reliving infinitely.

"[Y]our one duty is to live and be happy," (38) Zagreus tells Mersault; that such a philosophy of striving for personal "happiness" is apolitical is undeniable, even with the novel's implicit critique of the degrading effects of poverty. And, certainly, more recent theories of overtly and aggressively politicized subjectivity, which we will discuss in the next chapter, emphasize other duties that override self-interest. But it is worth recognizing the continuing utility of Nietzsche's, Sartre's, and Camus's injunctions: "Happiness implied a choice, and within that choice a concerted will, a lucid desire. He could hear Zagreus: 'Not the will to renounce, but the will to happiness'" (Camus 1972: 118). That emphasis on inner transformation, the taking of responsibility, and the active construction of a meaningful purpose certainly shifts the emphasis in a potentially politicized or politicizable way from a passive acceptance of circumstances to an energetic grappling with them. Thus Sartre, in distinguishing his own methods from those of Freudians, states that his purpose is "to bring to light, in a strictly objective form, the subjective choice by which each living person makes himself a person; that is, makes known to himself what he is" (Sartre 1992: 734). Yet he also foregrounds the political implications inherent in the existentialist perspective:

> when once a man has seen that values depend upon himself, in that state of forsakenness he can will only one thing, and that is freedom as the foundation of all values. That does not mean that he wills it in the abstract. . . . A man who belongs to some communist or revolutionary society wills certain concrete ends, which imply the will to freedom, but that freedom is willed in community. We will freedom for freedom's sake, in and through particular circumstances. And in thus willing freedom, we discover that it depends entirely upon the freedom of others and that the freedom of others depends upon our own.
>
> (Sartre 1975: 366)

Thus existentialism complements other theories' and theorists' explicit calls for politicization with its reminder that our processing of our lives and contexts, the theoretical frames that we bring to bear on them, are at least somewhat under our own control. The precise degree of control remains a much contested notion, but no recent theory of subjectivity countenances abject stasis or wholesale powerlessness even in emphasizing the socio-cultural forces that construct us. Agency over our own happiness and selfhood remains the elusive goal, even when selfhood and happiness are collectively defined and that agency is seen as thoroughly compromised.

3

THE POLITICS OF IDENTITY

LACAN

In the remaining chapters, we will be examining the wide range of theoretical perspectives and methodological interests that have animated discussions of subjectivity, identity, and political agency in the past half century. These build on, diverge from, and otherwise operate dialogically vis-à-vis the theories and articulations explored in preceding chapters. Their terms and intents certainly vary and can even clash, but the goal often remains some form of demonstrable, even if slippery, empowerment, if not over selfhood itself, then over the concept of selfhood as a means of cultural critical analysis. For many theorists of late, the text of the self offers a particularly important entry point into discussions of the textuality of culture and human social interaction.

The work of the French psychoanalytic theorist Jacques Lacan (1901–1981) epitomizes this palpable shift from outright attempts to exert control *over* subjectivity to attempts to use the concept of subjectivity as the occasion for much broader exercises in analysis. Lacan both lauded Freud's insights and departed from them, shifting the psychoanalytic discussion away from pathologization and normalization to the use value of psychoanalytic concepts in iconoclastic cultural interpretation.

This is signaled clearly in Lacan's caustic references to the role of the psychoanalyst and what he terms the "institution" of Freudian theory. He notes, "I am not saying . . . that the psycho-analytic community is a Church. Yet the question indubitably does arise – what is it in that community that is so reminiscent of religious practice?" (Lacan 1981: 4). Lacan rejects the notion of the analyst as purveyor of "truth": "there is nothing doctrinal about our office. We are answerable to no ultimate truth; we are neither for nor against any particular religion" (Lacan 1977: 316). In his 1953–54 seminar on *Freud's Papers on Technique* he answers the question of whether or not analysts should "push [their] subjects on the road of absolute knowledge" with "Certainly not . . . It is not our function to guide them by the hand through life" (Lacan 1991a: 265). As his biographer, Elisabeth Roudinesco, notes, "Jacques Lacan sought to bring plague, subversion, and disorder to the moderate Freudianism of his time" (Roudinesco 1997: xv). She later adds, "According to Lacan, psychoanalysis can never be an agent in the adaptation of man to society" (216). Indeed, Lacan writes: "Psycho-analysis is neither a *Weltanschauung*, nor a philosophy that claims to provide a key to the universe. It is governed by a particular aim, which is historically defined by the elaboration of the notion of the subject. It poses this notion in a new way, by leading the subject back to his signifying dependence" (Lacan 1981: 77).

One other aspect of Lacan's departure from Freud is important to mention here initially, for it is justly famous. While Freud's emphasis on the hidden causes for aberrant or anti-social activities led him to posit a theory of the unconscious as a repository of unfulfilled desires and unfinished processes, Lacan was less interested in pathologizing certain desires or activities and much more concerned with broadly interpreting the structuring principles of social identity and then pointing out how its debris becomes lodged in the unconscious. His famous assertion and rejoinder to Freud is that "the unconscious is structured like a language" (Lacan 1981: 203); indeed, the always partial and imperfect nature of linguistic interaction means that proscribed or simply messy meanings and implications must be denied, even if they continue to haunt us. As we shall see, Lacan continued to emphasize that to understand human behavior one must grapple with the rules and processes of human communication. He thereby replaces the social scientific emphasis on normalization in the psychoanalytic community with a cultural critical emphasis on the discovery of the underlying processes whereby the norm is established and maintained.

We can note here only a few of the many aspects of Lacanian theory that concern subjectivity; most germane are those that dovetail with the issue of agency that we will continue to explore. Indeed, to what end or ends do we attempt to exercise agency over our own and others' subjectivity? Lacan actually uses the desire for and illusion of control over selfhood as one of the bases of his theory of human developmental psychology. In Lacan's theory of the mirror stage, the infant is confronted with her or his own image in the mirror; that image provides both an illusion of a complete and controllable being that is the "self," and also sense of irresolvable tension given the infant's continuing experience of its body as always fragmented and incomplete: "the sight alone of the whole form of the human body gives the subject an imaginary mastery over his body . . . [one] which entirely structures his fantasy life" (Lacan 1991a: 79). Sometimes used literally and other times metaphorically by Lacan, the concept of the "mirror stage" points to the continuing human desire for self-sufficiency and agency that is always dialectically bound with, and undercut by, feelings of powerlessness and fragmentation: "the *mirror stage* is based on the relation between . . . tendencies which are experienced . . . as disconnected, discordant, in pieces . . . and a unity with which it is merged and paired. It is in this unity that the subject for the first time knows himself as a unity, but as an alienated, virtual unity" (Lacan 1991b: 50). Lacan sums up: the subject "only perceives the unity of this specific image from the outside, and in an anticipated manner. Because of this double relation which he has with himself, all the objects of his world are always structured around the wandering shadow of his own ego" (Lacan 1991b: 166).

This tension, between control and fragmentation, is only imperfectly assuaged by our subsequent developmental encounter with language, or what Lacan more broadly terms the "symbolic order." That term is used by Lacan to refer to all means by which we communicate and make, as well as replicate, meaning. In the Lacanian perspective, our very "selves" are created through language: "The form in which language is expressed itself defines subjectivity . . . I identify myself in language, but only by losing myself in it like an object" (Lacan 1977: 85–86). Yet central also to Lacan's theories is the illusion of wholeness and mastery that language provides:

> Symbols in fact envelop the life of man in a network so total that . . . they bring to his birth, along with the gifts of the stars, if not the gifts of the fairies, the shape of his destiny; so total that they give the words that will make him faithful or renegade, the law of the acts that will follow him right to the very place where he is not yet and even beyond his death; and so total that through them his end finds its meaning in the last judgment, where the Word absolves his being or condemns it.
>
> (Lacan 1977: 68)

Our immersion into the symbolic, as we acquire language and our identity through language in early childhood, serves thus as a balm assuaging our fragmentation; however, it also engenders innumerable new tensions as language itself is notoriously unreliable and unfixed/unfixable:

> All human beings share in the universe of symbols. They are included in it and submit to it, much more than they constitute it. They are much more its supports than its agents. It is as a function of the symbols, of the symbolic constitution of his history, that those variations are produced in which the subject is open to taking on the variable, broken, fragmented, sometimes even unconstituted and regressive, images of himself.
>
> (Lacan 1991a: 157–58)

In all of its many aspects, then, Lacan's theory of subjectivity is one of inherent vacillation and unsteadiness in the face of a continuing desire for a firm grounding and sense of security:

> The symbolic function presents itself as a double movement within the subject: man makes an object of his action, but only in order to restore to this action in due time its place as a grounding. In this equivocation, operating at every instant, lies the whole process of a function in which action and knowledge alternate.
>
> (Lacan 1977: 73)

This dynamic also underlies Lacan's perspective on agency, which is always grounded in tautologies but is no less necessary for being tautological. We create our groundings for action, which we need then to consider authentic: "what is realized in my history is not the past definite of what was, since it is no more, or even the present perfect of what has been in what I am, but the future anterior of what I shall have been for what I am in the process of becoming" (Lacan 1977: 86).

As slippery and notoriously difficult as Lacan's theories are, the commentary above still implies some possibility of agency and personal responsibility vis-à-vis subjectivity. He even offers a concrete example of a politically progressive grounding: "phase one, the man who works at the level of production in our society considers himself as belonging to the proletariat; phase two, in the name of belonging to it, he joins in a general strike" (Lacan 1977: 74). In "the brazen face of capitalist exploitation" (Lacan 1977: 74), he suggests, our tautologies, our chosen groundings, can be politically progressive ones. Lacan never suggests that we should be apolitical or resigned to indeterminacy and/or incapacity; instead, he avers, "There's absolutely no reason why we should make ourselves the guarantors of the bourgeois dream. A little more rigor and firmness are required in our confrontation with the human condition" (Lacan 1997: 303). In fact, his is a form of agency and political attachment that derives from disturbing the self-satisfaction of any belief in having arrived at ultimate truths or rational self-mastery: "the philosophical *cogito* is at the center of the mirage that renders modern man so sure of being himself even in his uncertainties about himself" (Lacan 1997: 165). He writes in *Seminar XI*, "I will now dare to define the Cartesian *I think* as participating, in its striving towards certainty, in a sort of abortion" (Lacan 1981: 141). As Roudinesco notes, "what was of supreme importance in Lacan's system was the elucidation of the individual's relation to the truth" (206). By denaturalizing and thoroughly disturbing that relation, Lacan opened up the possibility for *different* relations. Yannis Stavrakakis in *Lacan and the Political* argues that Lacan's work has a myriad of possible implications for political theory, as it "recognizes the division of citizens' identities and the fluidity of their political persuasions. In fact it points to the lack in the subject, to a conception of subjectivity which is not unified by reference to a single positive principle" (Stavrakakis 1991: 129).

Not surprisingly, Lacan was intrigued by literary and aesthetic representations of fluidity and metamorphosis, states imperfect and ambiguous, that unsettle our notions of the natural, the fixed, and the complete. This offers one avenue for the use of Lacan in literary and cultural analysis. Lacan explores the always-threatening return of fragmentation, however our adult identity may be secured, in his attention to "imagos of the fragmented body": "images of castration, mutilation, dismemberment, dislocation, evisceration, devouring, bursting open of the body" (Lacan 1977: 11). He notes specifically, "We must turn to the works of Hieronymus Bosch for an atlas of all the aggressive images that torment mankind" (Lacan 1977: 11).

> This fragmented body . . . usually manifests itself in dreams when the movement of analysis encounters a certain level of aggressive disintegration in the individual. It then appears in the form of disjointed limbs, or of those organs represented in exoscopy, growing wings and taking up arms for intestinal persecutions – the very same that the visionary Hieronymous Bosch has fixed, for all time, in painting, in the ascent from the fifteenth century to the imaginary zenith of modern man.
>
> (Lacan 1977: 4–5)

Slavoj Zizek, Lacan's foremost critical proponent today, also makes this link in his concept of the Lacanian "Monstrous": "a pre-ontological universe of the 'night of the world' in which partial objects wander in a state preceding any synthesis, like that in Hieronymus Bosch's paintings (which are strictly correlative to the emergence of modern subjectivity)" (Zizek 1999: 49–50). While not mentioned by name, Bosch's "The Garden of Delights" (c.1514–16) is no doubt the basis for the commentary above; in it we find bodies, half-formed and deformed, jumbles of limbs, and body parts alone and in shocking combination. Bosch therein reveals the base-level fear of fragmentation that drives human attempts to secure identity, "to identify with something external, other, different, in order to acquire the basis of a self-unified identity" (Stavrakakis 1991: 18). The Lacanian recognition of the fragmented undercurrent to subjectivity helps explain the tenacity with which many people cling to rigid ideologies, religion, and structures of nationalism and fascism.

An even more direct corollary can be found in the paintings of Salvador Dalí (1904–89), whom Lacan knew and whose images have numerous political and identity political implications. In "Soft Construction with Boiled Beans – Premonition of Civil War" (1936), Dalí makes a clear link between the impartial, fragmented body and the horrific grip of fascism, depicted as muscular and talon-like. In this image, a hate-distorted visage sits atop a structure of disjointed and partially formed, yet still sinewy and firmly planted, limbs. Ascending to the sky above a wasteland, this solid architectural structure links the rise of fascism to fears of bodily dissolution and incoherence. Dalí and Lacan both allow a potentially identity-altering insight into the roots of human violence and destruction, pointing not toward a neat trajectory of healing or normalization, but nevertheless challenging us to find different ways of living with fear or inherent fragmentation.

Indeed, however tenuous our grasp on coherence and identity may be, Lacan urges us toward an intellectually quickened stance, one of more "rigor" and "firmness," in theorizing that "Division and disharmony are constitutive of the human condition" (Stavrakakis 1991: 136) and that only through radical forms of political understanding and engagement can we mediate "between universalism and particularism in achieving a non-totalitarian sense of social unity" (Lacan 1977: 137). Lacan sums up, "What we teach the subject to recognize as his unconscious is his history – that is to say, we help him to perfect the present historicization of the facts that have already determined a certain number of the historical 'turning-points' of his existence" (Lacan 1977: 52). In so critically regarding the past and present, Lacan opens up the future also to radical revisionary engagement.

ALTHUSSER

Lacan lived and wrote during a time of intense intellectual production in France. Among his circle of acquaintances and someone with whom he shared both ideas and commitments was Louis Althusser (1918–90). Althusser provided several important new analytical concepts to the ongoing twentieth-century discussion of subjectivity, especially concerning the intersection of class critique and psychoanalytic interpretation. As James Kavanagh notes,

Contemporary Marxist theory, deriving largely from the work of Louis Althusser, has reworked the concept of ideology in the light of the more complex notion of subject-formation given by psychoanalysis, and the more elaborate system of ideological practices that have developed in late capitalist societies. In this framework, ideology designates a rich "system of representations," worked up in specific material practices, which helps form individuals into social subjects who "freely" internalize an appropriate "picture" of their social world and their place in it. Ideology offers the social subject not a set of narrowly "political" ideas but a fundamental framework of assumptions that defines the parameters of the real and the self; it constitutes what Althusser calls the social subject's "'lived' relation to the real."

(Kavanagh 1995: 310)

Althusser offers a trenchant analysis of how belief systems reproduce, as they, in effect, *seduce* new subjects.

Kavanagh remarks that "We now understand this process of 'subjection' as working largely through an address to unconscious fears and desires as well as rational interests, and we understand it as working through a multiplicity of disparate, complexly interconnected social apparatuses" (310). Indeed, Althusser offered a new vocabulary for understanding both the direct and indirect means by which human thought and activity are brought into conformity with general social definitions and norms. The most direct means are those of "Repressive State Apparatuses" or RSAs: "the police, the courts, the prisons; but also the army . . . and above this ensemble, the head of State, the government and the administration" (Althusser 1971: 137). RSAs function "'by violence', . . . massively and predominantly *by repression* (including physical repression)" (145). We all encounter RSAs and their restrictive force regularly, in our acknowledgment and conformity to the dictates of police officers, passport control officials, judges, and tax collectors.

Yet even more insidious and certainly much harder to gain a critical distance from are what Althusser terms "Ideological State Apparatuses" or ISAs. These work covertly to nurture and cajole a "submission to the rules of established order" (132), and include:

the religious ISA (the system of different Churches), the educational ISA (the system of the different public and private "Schools"), the family ISA, the legal ISA, the political ISA (the political system, including the different Parties), the trade-union ISA, the communications ISA (press, radio and television, etc.), the cultural ISA (Literature, the Arts, sports, etc.).

(143)

ISAs function by passing along, and passing off as natural and unchallengeable, the fundamental belief systems of a society. This is no simple top-down model of oppression, for both oppressors and oppressed are acculturated into their proper roles. The reproduction of a class structure, Althusser notes, requires not only "a reproduction of submission to the ruling ideology for the workers, [but also] a reproduction of the ability to manipulate the ruling ideology correctly for the agents of exploitation and repression" (132–33). Althusser thus shifted dramatically the focus for discussions of subjectivity onto the veiled mechanisms by which all individuals acquire their sense of place and purpose in society.

Althusser offers an intriguing but controversial metaphor for precisely how this occurs: that of interpellation. According to Althusser's theory of social construction, we are "hailed" by ideology much as we might be called to on the street by a member of the police force; we respond to the call unwittingly, even automatically, and acquire thereby our subjectivity in relationship to prevailing social definitions and categories. He sums up:

In the ordinary use of the term, subject in fact means: (1) a free subjectivity, a center of initiatives, author of and responsible for its actions; (2) a subjected being, who submits to a higher authority, and is therefore stripped of all freedom except that of freely accepting his submission. [In fact] the individual *is interpellated as a (free) subject in order that he shall submit freely to the commandments of the Subject, i.e. in order that he shall (freely) accept his subjection*, i.e. in order that he shall make the gestures and actions of his subjection "all by himself." *There are no subjects except by and for their subjection.*

(182, original emphasis)

By "Subject" in this passage, Althusser means an absolute, central, meaning-giving device, such as God or a replacement lynchpin such as capitalism or nationalism. Amalgamating Lacanian and Marxist theories, he suggests that we seek in relationship to that Subject a sense of security and validation in the ongoing human experience of fragmentation, uncontrollability, and unpredictability. "Lacan," Althusser writes, "demonstrates the effectiveness of the Order, the Law, that has been lying in wait for each infant born since before his birth, and seizes him before his first cry, assigning to him his place and role, and hence his fixed destination" (211). "Hegemony" is the related term used by the theorist Antonio Gramsci (1891–1937) to convey the extent to which belief systems are thoroughly naturalized and deeply dominate the consciousnesses of individuals, who think they submit freely to the reigning economic and political system but who are more or less programmed to do so.

But where, in this schema, is there any possibility for human agency or social change? As Tony Davies notes in *Humanism*, Lacanian and Althusserian theory

> kicks away the twin pillars of humanism: the sovereignty of rational conscious, and the authenticity of individual speech. I do not think, I am thought. You do not speak, you are spoken. Thought and speech, which for the humanist had been the central substance of identity, are located elsewhere, and the self is a vacancy. . . . Thus, for Althusser, the "subject" of history is not the individual human being, speaking and acting purposefully in a world illuminated by rational freedom, but the impersonal "structure in dominance" – what Marx called the "forces and relations in production" that "operate outside man and independent of his will," and that set the pattern and horizon of individual action.
>
> (Davies 1997: 60)

This leads Terry Eagleton to decry what he terms the "political bleakness of Althusser's theory" (Eagleton 1991: 145); Eagleton sums up, "For [Althusser] subjectivity itself would seem just a form of self-incarceration; and the question of where political resistance springs from must thus remain obscure" (146).

But other critics and theorists find Althusser far less defeatist and politically deflating. Judith Butler, for instance, argues that Althusser's scene of "interpellation" should be considered "exemplary and allegorical" (Butler 1997: 106), and that our conscription in and through that scene is always partial and open to challenge: "we might reread 'being' as precisely the potentiality that remains unexhausted by any particular interpellation" (131). And out of a recognition of the seductive power of interpellation, comes the possibility of critique and other forms of agency:

> For the "I" to launch its critique, it must first understand that the "I" itself is dependent upon its complicitous desire for the law to make possible its own existence. A critical review of the law will not, therefore, undo the force of conscience unless the one who offers that critique is willing, as it were, to be undone by the critique that he or she performs.
>
> (106)

Granted, Butler's is a broad, rather than a strict and literal, use of Althusser, yet she certainly helps us understand why his concepts remain so compelling even if they have been widely criticized. Althusserian theory lends itself to practical critical interpretation, both of cultural processes and of literary texts, and that is a manifestation of the political resistance that Eagleton finds so hard to locate. Kavanagh suggests a direct political benefit offered by Althusserian analysis, in that it challenges "the institutional and/or textual apparatuses that work on the reader's or spectator's imaginary conceptions of self and social order [as they] call or *solicit* (or 'interpellate,' as Althusser puts it . . .) him/her into a specific form of social 'reality' and social subjectivity" (310). Even Eagleton recognizes, in *Marxism and Literary Criticism*, that an Althusserian criticism might usefully "seek to explain the literary work in terms of the ideological structure of which it is part, yet which it transforms in its art" (Eagleton 1976: 19).

Needless to say, we can perform such criticism with any type of text as our focus, but one particularly appropriate and intriguing object of analysis worth mentioning here is children's literature since it is not only part of prior ideological structures, as all texts are, but is often blatantly didactic, offered and even marketed as a mechanism for the interpellation of the child into her or his adult social identity. Indeed, it is interesting to note which texts have become widely used as children's literature, even if they originally met the needs of a much broader audience. Fairy tales, for example, are now marketed almost solely as children's texts, obscuring their origins in folk and oral culture. The tales collected by Charles Perrault in France in the late seventeenth century and the Brothers Grimm in Germany in the early nineteenth century have become firmly established as part of the canon of children's literature classics. This is hardly surprising when we consider their interpellative power, especially in reproducing gender ideologies. "The Sleeping Beauty," for example, offers an image of feminine desirability linked powerfully to passivity and aesthetic objectification. "Cinderella," too, differentiates clearly between the evil sisters who are aggressive and querulous and the idealized Cinderella who is meek, quietly industrious, and ever-so-dainty. "Snow White" combines aspects of the two narratives just mentioned; she first proves herself blissful in domesticity with the dwarves and then thoroughly dependent for her life upon the rescuing power of her handsome prince. The translation of these and other tales into enormously popular animated films by Disney in the mid-twentieth century means that their messages concerning feminine passivity and domesticity have continued to work to interpellate generations of girls even to this day.

Of course boys are also interpellated by such works. All of the tales and films above convey powerful cultural expectations concerning masculine attributes and behaviors. In and through them, boys are told that they must be brave, strong, and, of course, heterosexual. In fact, Disney's 1942 animated film *Bambi* is as rigid in its conveyance of proper and improper male gender roles as Disney's *Cinderella* and *Snow White* are in their messages to women. As I have argued elsewhere (Hall 1996b), its title character moves from an androgynous, emotional, and self-questioning "boyhood" to a narrowly defined performance of adult, male heterosexuality as the patriarch of the forest in the film's final scene. As Bambi experiences and overcomes the emotional trauma of the loss of his mother and learns to direct his desires toward a suitable mate (leaving behind his boyhood pals), he is formed socially into a copy of his father, the old forest ruler, and comes to embody all of the attributes deemed desirable in men in post-World War II America. He is the aloof bread-winner who juts out his chest and calmly surveys his domestic kingdom in the film's final image.

Even though a male character such as Bambi is clearly empowered socially and politically when compared to the domestically confined heroines of other Disney classics, the roles and behaviors it glorifies are still highly restrictive, as it conditions boys into conformity to the needs of reproduction-based, capitalist society. And while such films are certainly intriguing for their historical insight into mid-twentieth-century gender ideologies, perhaps even more worthy of critical consideration is the fact that they are not museum pieces. They continue to circulate widely as video rentals and in innumerable family video collections across the globe, and thereby continue to function as part of the cultural ISA, working to mold young girls and boys into their adult gender roles (as well as those of class, race, and national identity). While certainly alternate gender ideologies are now perceptible in children's film, television, and print culture, we should hardly wonder at the slowness with which norms such as those of masculinity and femininity metamorphose. Twenty-first century children are still being hailed powerfully by the blatantly sexist belief systems of decades and even centuries past.

FOUCAULT AND DISCOURSE THEORY

We now come to one of the most controversial and certainly the most influential recent theorist of subjectivity: Michel Foucault (1926–84). Many of the objections raised concerning Althusser's theories of the social construction of identity and the seemingly meager possibilities for agency implied therein have been directed even more intensely at Foucault's theories. Terry Eagleton terms Foucault's terminologies and theses "politically toothless" (Eagleton 1991: 7) and states that "even more glaringly for Michel Foucault" than for Althusser, "subjectivity itself would seem just a form of self-incarceration" (146). Max Kirsch is more critical still, saying that for Foucault and related theorists, "politics" has "no inherent meaning" (Kirsch 2000: 9), and that the "individual and social action is rendered indiscernible" (23) in their work.

Others disagree. In *Disciplining Foucault: Feminism, Power, and the Body* Jana Sawicki maintains that "Foucault was one of the most politically engaged" of recent theorists and that his "books were intended to serve as [political] interventions in contemporary practices that govern the lives of oppressed groups" (Sawicki 1991: 95). In answer to those who claim that Foucault's theories "effectively robbed people of freedom and made successful political opposition impossible," David Halperin notes that Foucault's *History of Sexuality, Volume I* was widely and explicitly identified by AIDS activists of the late 1980s as their "single most important intellectual source of political inspiration" (Halperin 1995: 15–16). Christopher Falzon adds that "the spirit, the driving force, behind [Foucault's] work, his overriding concern [was] to help challenge states of deadening imprisonment and to foster the emergence of new forms of thought and action" (Falzon 1998: 15).

In his effort to do so, Foucault rejected centuries-old assumptions concerning subjectivity. Rather than starting with the Enlightenment ideal of full self-knowledge and self-aware agency, Foucault shifts the critical focus onto "discourse," a broad concept that he uses to refer to language and other forms of representation – indeed, all human mechanisms for the conveyance of meaning and value. Tony Davies draws some useful analogies with some of the theorists whom we have already discussed:

> *Discourse* for Foucault is what the relations of production are for Marx, the unconscious for Freud, the impersonal laws of language for Saussure, ideology for Althusser: the capillary structure of social cohesion and conformity. It situates us as individuals, and silently legislates the boundaries of what is possible for us to think and say. Above all, it is normative: not because transgression and dissent are impossible . . . but because they too are "grammatical," already anticipated and positioned in the hegemonic syntax of discursive power.
>
> (Davies 1997: 70)

In his lecture "The Discourse on Language," Foucault asserts that in "every society the production of discourse is at once controlled, selected, organized and redistributed," that however "humdrum and grey [this] may seem," "behind these words" lies a myriad of "conflicts, triumphs, injuries, dominations and enslavements" (Foucault 1972: 216). Indeed, it is that multifaceted and multivalent relationship between power and discourse that is the subject of Foucault's most intense intellectual interest.

In an encyclopedia entry that he wrote about himself under a pseudonym, Foucault summarizes his philosophical project:

> to study the constitution of the subject as an object for himself: the formation of the procedures by which the subject is led to observe himself, analyze himself, interpret himself, recognize himself as a domain of possible knowledge. In short, this concerns the history of "subjectivity," if what is meant by that term is the way in which the subject experiences himself in a game of truth where he relates to himself.
>
> (Foucault 1998: 461)

As the most thoroughgoing of social constructionists, Foucault asserts that we can only come to know our "selves" through historically specific (and differentially valued) categories of truth, propriety, and normality. He suggests,

> In regard to human nature or the categories that may be applied to the subject, everything in our knowledge which is suggested to us as being universally valid must be tested and analyzed. . . . [We must] circumvent the anthropological universals (and, of course, those of a humanism that would assert the rights, the privileges, and that nature of a human being as an immediate and timeless truth of the subject) in order to examine them as historical constructs.
>
> (461–62)

In books on the social construction of madness, the penal system, and sexuality, among other topics, written over the course of three decades, Foucault examined the "historically singular mode[s] of experience in which the subject is objectified for himself and for others through certain specific procedures of 'government'" (463).

Admittedly, Foucault's use of the term "government" in the quotation above seems to indicate a pessimistic view of the individual's relationship to broader flows of social power. However, Foucault's perspective is actually much more complicated than that, for he suggests repeatedly that power is never exercised in a top-down fashion. Power circulates, is appropriated and deployed, and requires a multidimensional model to grasp it in its complexity. His notion of the "polyvalence of discourses" helps address that need. In *The History of Sexuality, Volume I*, he asserts, famously,

> Discourses are not once and for all subservient to power or raised up against it. . . . We must make allowance for the complex and unstable process whereby discourse can be both an instrument and an effect of power, but also a hindrance, a stumbling-block, a point of resistance and a starting point for an opposing strategy. Discourse transmits and produces power; it reinforces it, but also undermines and exposes it, renders it fragile and makes it possible to thwart it.
>
> (Foucault 1990: 100–01)

His clearest example is of the category of the "homosexual" that arose during the nineteenth century:

> There is no question that the appearance in nineteenth-century psychiatry, jurisprudence, and literature of a whole series of discourses on the species and subspecies of homosexuality, inversion, pederasty, and "psychic hermaphrodism" made possible a strong advance of social controls into this area of "perversity"; but it also made possible the formation of a "reverse" discourse: homosexuality began to speak in its own behalf, to demand that its legitimacy or "naturality" be acknowledged, often in the same vocabulary, using the same categories by which it was medically disqualified.
>
> (101)

Thus Foucault's explicitly non-essentialist perspective on "power" is hardly pessimistic. Power is always circumscribed within historically specific terms and limits, but it is also always available for appropriation. To those theorists who need to imagine a possible transcendence of historical categories, a pure moment (and a vocabulary) of "liberation," Foucault may appear cynical or resigned. But Foucault himself was always politically engaged and repeatedly urged others to political action. In his important essay from 1982 "The Subject and Power," he even offers an explicit challenge to his readers concerning a possible deployment of power over their own subjectivities:

> Maybe the target nowadays is not to discover what we are but to refuse what we are. We have to imagine and to build up what we could be to get rid of this kind of political "double bind," which is the simultaneous individualization and totalization of modern power structures.
>
> The conclusion would be that the political, ethical, social, philosophical problem of our days is not to try to liberate the individual from the state, and from the state's institutions, but to liberate us both from the state and from the type of individualization linked to the state. We have to promote new forms of subjectivity through the refusal of this kind of individuality that has been imposed on us for several centuries.
>
> (Foucault 2000: 336)

Foucault never delineates the precise new form that subjectivity would take, nor does he predict some utopian moment of full self-knowledge or empowerment over our selves. Instead he calls for critically examining old templates and proliferating the possibilities for different forms and manifestations of subjectivity in the future. Thus Foucauldian critics and theorists of the past two decades argue that one does not necessarily need a point of pure outside perspective on power to gain some leverage over its flows and instances of regulation. To recognize that we are always caught up in the notions, terms, and values of our day does not lead inevitably to quietism or defeatism in our relationship to them. But it certainly should dislodge our assumption of mastery over them and any smugness that we may have concerning our own truths and critical formulae.

Judith Butler is perhaps the most important recent critic and theorist who finds in Foucault a clear political dynamism. In *The Psychic Life of Power*, she writes:

> For Foucault, the subject who is produced through subjection is

not produced at an instant in its totality. Instead, it is in the process of being produced, it is repeatedly produced (which is not the same as being produced again and again). It is precisely the possibility of a repetition which does not consolidate the dissociated unity, the subject, but which proliferates effects which undermine the force of normalization.

(Butler 1997: 93)

While I will return to Butler's theories shortly, it is important to recognize her point here, that "The Foucaultian subject is never fully constituted in subjection" (94), that Foucault does not suggest that discourse turns us into automatons. If that were the case, where would political disagreement – as it has always existed – come from? Indeed, where would Foucault, with all of his iconoclasm, come from? Falzon, in his *Foucault and Social Dialogue*, adds his voice to Butler's, saying that for Foucault, "there will always be resistance, revolt, struggle against social imposed constraints, renewed dialogue and the transformation of social forms. The agent of change here is the concrete, resisting human being" (Falzon 1998: 52).

The Foucaultian perspective on possibilities for agency within and against prevailing discourses can also serve to energize applied literary and cultural criticism. It prods us to examine "texts" as instances of discursive production and possibly pointed and effective resistance. While Foucault's insights were clearly bound up with the political and philosophical interests and language of the late twentieth century, a critical perspective on time-bound categories and historically specific, differential valuations can traced back to the beginnings of identity politics, as we saw in our overview of early challenges to naturalized oppression on the basis of race and gender. Thus many texts from previous eras might lend themselves to Foucaultian analysis even if they also demonstrate inevitably their own time-bound qualities. One possibility from the relatively near past is Virginia Woolf's 1928 novel *Orlando* in which the eponymous hero/heroine not only changes biological sex over the centuries, but also experiences profound shifts in gender definitions and gendered modes of existence as discourse changes over time. Soon after she awakens one morning to discover that she has suddenly, mysteriously become a woman, Orlando finds herself:

becoming a little more modest, as women are, of her brains, and a little more vain, as women are, of her person. Certain susceptibilities were asserting themselves, and others were diminishing. The change of clothes had, some philosophers will say, much to do with it. Vain trifles as they seem, clothes have, they say, more important offices than merely to keep us warm. They change our view of the world and the world's view of us. For example, when Captain Bartolus saw Orlando's skirt, he had an awning stretched for her immediately, pressed her to take another slice of beef, and invited her to go ashore with him in the long boat. These compliments would certainly not have been paid her had her skirts, instead of flowing, been cut tight to her legs in the fashion of breeches. And when we are paid compliments, it behooves us to make some return. Orlando curtseyed; she complied, she flattered the good man's humours as she would not have done had his neat breeches been a woman's skirts, and his braided coat a woman's satin bodice. Thus, there is much to support the view that it is clothes that wear us and not we them; we may make them take the mould of arm or breast; but they mould our hearts, our brains, our tongues to their liking.

(Woolf 1956: 187–88)

Half a century before Foucault articulated his thoroughgoing social constructionist theories, we find here startling insight into the effect of that gendered discourse on behavior and the expression of selfhood. Clothing, a manifestation of gendered discourse, has a subtle but powerful effect on our subjectivities. Woolf reveals that however much we may think we mold discourse, it also inevitably molds us. As the novel moves through centuries of time, *Orlando* explores the profound changes in the ways that gender has been expressed during different eras and how historically contingent definitions of proper and improper behavior become internalized and naturalized as the parameters of our selfhoods.

Yet, as we traced above, Foucault did not suggest that social definitions are simply imprinted on passive subjects, he also recognized the many ways individuals respond within prevailing discourses. *Orlando* is not the best example of that Foucaultian interest, but certainly numerous texts from the highly politicized latter half of the twentieth century do offer ample opportunities for analysis. For example, Gwendolyn Brooks's poem "Boy Breaking Glass" from 1968 takes the instance of an inner city, African American youth committing a mundane act of vandalism, throwing a rock through a window pane, as an occasion for musing on subjectivity. Brooks explores how an economically and socially disadvantaged individual, "Who has not Congress, lobster, love, luau,/the Regency Room, the Statue of Liberty," finds a mode of self-expression and highly compromised and problematic empowerment: "I shall create! If not a note, a hole./If not an overture, a desecration." The point of the poem, of course, is not simply to describe a process of oppression and frustrated response, but also to urge broader forms of political change. Indeed, both Brooks and Foucault were participants in a late twentieth-century discussion of the need for radical social change, suggesting that subjectivity originates in flows of social power and historical legacies of differential valuations. When "The only sanity is a cup of tea," as Brooks writes, the heavily biased, class specific notion of what counts as "sane" is revealed in striking fashion, and her implicit challenge to readers is to critically examine and radically alter oppressive definitions, tendentious social categories, and our normal points of reference and value.

THE POLITICS OF GENDER AND SEXUALITY

That discussion of how the *norm* differently impacts upon groups of people has been particularly intense in the field of gender and sexuality studies. Indeed, late twentieth-century theories of gender and sexual identity have drawn from, intersected with, and enriched many of the other theories that we have discussed in preceding pages. Some feminist and gender theories begin with a deliberate departure from Freud; others explicitly reference, and sometimes pointedly diverge from, Lacanian, Althusserian, and Foucaultian perspectives. But to approach feminist theory in this way, as derivative and as a field of knowledge defined solely by its relationship to theories articulated by men, would be to ignore the fact that it has been a central theoretical force in the twentieth century, in and of itself. Here, instead, I will point to some of the most important theories of and perspectives on gender and subjectivity, and sexuality and subjectivity, from the last half century, highlighting the *centrality* of the insights that they have offered on identity politics and the question of agency and selfhood.

In her succinct, sometimes polemical, overview of twentieth-century feminist theory, *Sexual/Textual Politics*, Toril Moi states with characteristic aplomb: "Simone de Beauvoir is surely the greatest feminist theorist of our time" (Moi 1985: 91). While I am always skeptical of such cut-and-dry statements, certainly it is important to recognize that Beauvoir (1908–86) brought to the discussion of gender oppression an intense intellectual energy and excitement, and she contributed importantly to mid-century philosophical debates concerning knowledge and being. As Moi notes, Beauvoir's central thesis in *The Second Sex* (1949), is that:

> throughout history, . . . "woman" has been constructed as man's Other, denied the right to her own subjectivity and to responsibility for her own actions. . . . [W]omen themselves internalize this objectified vision, thus living in a constant state of "inauthenticity" or "bad faith," as Sartre might have put it. The fact that women often enact the roles patriarchy has prescribed for them does not prove that patriarchal analysis is right: Beauvoir's uncompromising refusal of any notion of a female nature or essence is succinctly summed up in her famous statement "One is not born a woman; one becomes one."
>
> (Moi 1985: 92)

Moi rightly distinguishes Beauvoir as the proponent of an aggressively constructionist approach to women's subjectivity. According to Beauvoir, women's roles and behaviors reflect indelibly the fact that woman "is defined and differentiated with reference to man and not he with reference to her; she is the incidental, the inessential as opposed to the essential. He is the Subject, he is the Absolute – she is the Other" (Beauvoir 1974: xix). Women are thus acculturated into their roles in ways that are very difficult to challenge or change: "woman may fail to lay claim to the status of subject because she lacks definite resources, because she feels the necessary bond that ties her to man regardless of reciprocity, and because she is often very well pleased with her role as the *Other*" (xxiv–xxv). As Beauvoir notes, woman "stands before man not as a subject but as an object paradoxically endued with subjectivity; she takes herself simultaneously as *self* and as *other*, a contradiction that entails baffling consequences" (799). Much of succeeding feminist theory in the twentieth century will tackle directly this struggle to redefine women's subjectivity in ways that are less inherently derivative and that allow at least the *possibility* of agency in processes of *self*-construction or re-construction.

Indeed, the necessity of theorizing a form of subjectivity in which pre-existing and continuing *objectification* is not unalterable *determination* is why Catherine Belsey asserts, "One of the central issues for feminism is the cultural construction of subjectivity" (Belsey 1991: 593). For Julia Kristeva in "The Subject in Process" (1998), this means dismantling the Freudian "unitary subject" (133) and positing instead subjectivity always in the making and remaking, as desire is invested in "transformation itself" (159). Lacan is one of Kristeva's theoretical touchstones, for his emphasis on linguistic processes of subject formation allows her to posit also the recovery of pre-linguistic disruptions and alternate systems of meaning, even perhaps emanating from the interconnectedness between the pregnant woman and her unborn child. In this and other ways, Kristeva repudiates the use of the male body as the necessary standard against which women will be judged and their subjectivities always found lacking.

Belsey also briefly acknowledges both Lacan and Althusser to offer then her own perspective on how a woman can be "a *subjected being* who submits to the authority of the social formation represented in ideology as the Absolute Subject (God, the king, the boss, Man, conscience)" (Belsey 1991: 596), and yet also at times find agency and the ability to resist received roles and definitions. Like Kristeva, she focuses on "process" and possibilities for change therein:

> The subject is . . . the site of contradiction, and is consequently perpetually in the process of construction, thrown into crisis by alterations in language and in the social formation, capable of change. And in the fact that the subject is a *process* lies the possibility of transformation.
>
> In addition, the displacement of subjectivity across a range of discourses implies a range of positions from which the subject grasps itself and its relations with the real, and these positions may be incompatible or contradictory. It is these incompatibilities and contradictions

within what is taken for granted which exert a pressure on concrete individuals to seek new, non-contradictory subject-positions.

(597)

Belsey notes, "Women as a group in our society are both produced and inhibited by contradictory discourses. Very broadly, we participate both in the liberal-humanist discourse of freedom, self-determination and rationality and at the same time the specifically feminine discourse offered by society of submission, relative inadequacy and irrational intuition" (597–98). Belsey thus pinpoints the central contradiction that is subjectivity, as it simultaneously enables and inhibits. She follows other social constructionist theorists whom we have discussed here in her examination of "a dialectical relationship between concrete individuals and the language in which their subjectivity is constructed" (598). In fact, a focus on that process of social construction, in which the subject is not whole, but as unstable and fragmented as language itself, constitutes a specifically *poststructuralist* perspective on subjectivity, as we first saw in our discussion of Lacan.

Indeed, it is poststructuralism as a particularly productive avenue of philosophical inquiry that I am emphasizing here. In discussing gendered subjectivity, it certainly would be possible, and perhaps somewhat useful, to draw attention to *essentialist* theories concerning women's biologically or metaphysically based ways of knowing or being that differ essentially from those of men. Many sustained overviews of feminist theory, including Moi's as mentioned above, glance at those quickly. But the most supple and intellectually intriguing manifestations of feminist theory in its Anglo-American and Continental forms have at their base an engagement with the slippages and resistances that are possible notwithstanding the sometimes heavy weight of biology and naturalized definitions, roles, and behaviors. In fact, that potential elusiveness and changeability in gendered subjectivity is what makes Kristeva, however tactically she may reference the female body, a poststructuralist rather than a narrowly essentialist theorist. Thus Chris Weedon argues in *Feminist Practice and Poststructuralist Theory*:

The political significance of decentring the subject and abandoning the belief in essential subjectivity is that it opens up subjectivity to change. In making our subjectivity the product of the society and culture in which we live, feminist poststructuralism insists that forms of subjectivity are produced historically and change with shifts in the wide range of discursive fields which constitute them. However, feminist poststructuralism goes further than this to insist that the individual is always the site of conflicting forms of subjectivity.

(Weedon 1987: 33)

In drawing upon the work of Kristeva, Hélène Cixous, and numerous others, Weedon argues convincingly that

Although the subject in poststructuralism is social constructed in discursive practices, she none the less exists as a thinking, feeling subject and social agent, capable of resistance and innovations produced out of the clash between contradictory subject positions and practices. She is also a subject able to reflect upon the discursive relations which constitute her and the society in which she lives, and able to choose from the options available.

(125)

Thus Weedon, like most other feminist theorists of the last fifty years, works to account both for construction and contestation, for indeed, the tension between the two is inherent in subjectivity as it is defined in most considerations of the topic.

It is hardly surprising then that a poststructuralist theorist such as Diana Fuss would make opportunities for politicized response a key component of her work. In both *Essentially Speaking* (1989) and *Identification Papers* (1995), Fuss argues that categories both inhibit and empower, that a critical distance from, and careful use of, gender classifications and definitions offers one the ability to effect social change, for even "essentialism may have some strategic or interventionary value" if one remembers that "essence is a sign, and as such historically contingent and constantly subject to change and to redefinition" (Fuss 1989: 20). This meta-awareness never allows an instrumental control over subjectivity, but does allow avenues for contesting the categories of the normal and natural. In *Identification Papers*, Fuss focuses specifically on the process of iden-tifying with other individuals and with groups, arguing that identification is the "detour" that "defines a self," and as such, it "is a process that keeps identity at a distance, that prevents identity from ever approximating the status of an ontological given, even as it makes possible the formation of an illusion of identity as immediate, secure, and totalizable" (Fuss 1995: 2). This inside/outside movement is the political agent's only hope for effecting change, "working on the insides of our inherited sexual vocabularies and turning them inside out, giving them a new face" (Fuss 1991: 7).

This politicization of gendered subjectivity as a process, and site of plural definitions and resistances, allows us now to discuss the related, though not coterminous, field of sexual subjectivity theory that has also developed in the past few decades. As with the pointed departures of feminist theorists, so too have theorists of sexuality challenged Freud's influential narratives of normal development as they look for alternate models and possibilities for subject formation. Leo Bersani, in *The Freudian Body* (1986), decries how Freud "relentlessly pursues the project of domesticating and rationalizing the sexual in a historical narrative and a psychic structure" (102); heterosexuality is Freud's privileged norm against which adults will be judged in determining their relative mental health or illness. An equally dynamic challenge to Freud is issued by Gilles Deleuze and Felix Guattari, who in *Anti-Oedipus* (1983) look not to the unity of the normal heterosexual subject but to the disunity of the schizophrenic for a way of discussing desire that does not privilege bland conformity to the rules of middle-class domestic life. If language itself is a key mechanism of normalization, how is it possible ever to theorize *in language* an alternate model wherein what is considered abnormal is potentially revalued?

Indeed, "where does or can resistance come from?" is one of the most compelling intellectual questions of the past half-century. This returns us to Foucault, for as we observed earlier, the notion of a narrowly defined, normal sexual subjectivity is traceable to the mid- to late nineteenth century with the rise in medical classifications of health and illness and the drive to name, diagnose, and perhaps cure those sexual desires that deviated from reproduction-based heterosexual monogamy. Yet with this "appearance in nineteenth-century psychiatry, jurisprudence, and literature of a whole series of discourses on the species and subspecies of homosexuality, inversion, pederasty, and 'psychic hermaphrodism'"

(Foucault 1990: 101) came also a polyvalent reverse discourse of sexual self-identification and demands for recognition and legitimacy. While precursors of twentieth-century sexual subjectivities can be found throughout history (libertines and prostitutes, among others, sometimes thought of themselves, and were thought of, as having specifically sexual identities), the twentieth century saw a veritable explosion of new sexual subject positions and identity political movements that use received language differently and that require analysis in ways methodologically distinct even from feminist analysis.

Indeed, Gayle Rubin in her influential essay "Thinking Sex: Notes for a Radical Theory of the Politics of Sexuality" (1984), expands upon Foucault as she argues powerfully,

> The realm of sexuality . . . has its own internal politics, inequities, and modes of oppression. As with other aspects of human behavior, the concrete institutional forms of sexuality at any given time and place are products of human activity. They are imbued with conflicts of interest and political maneuvering, both deliberate and incidental. In that sense, sex is always political.
>
> (Rubin 1993: 4)

Rubin, a well-known feminist theorist, also makes the important point that "the relationship between feminism and sex is complex" (27–28), and that

> it is essential to separate gender and sexuality analytically to reflect more accurately their separate social existence. This goes against the grain of much contemporary feminist thought, which treats sexuality as a derivation of gender. For instance, lesbian feminist ideology has mostly analyzed the oppression of lesbians in terms of the oppression of women. However, lesbians are also oppressed as queers and perverts, by the operation of sexual, not gender, stratification.
>
> (33)

Rubin thus called for and helped lay the groundwork for "queer theory" as a theoretical domain interested specifically in sexual subjectivity and normativity. The early to mid-1990s saw then a flurry of activity in the theorization and creative abrasion of sexual subject positions, that, in Michael Warner's words, rejected "toleration or simple political interest-representation in favor of a more thorough resistance to regimes of the normal" (Warner 1993: xxvi). "Queer" became the useful, if controversial, umbrella term linking all whose critical work and/or daily practices abraded the notion of the sexually normal.

Judith Butler is perhaps the most important recent theorist who has attempted both to theorize and to queer (to undermine, de-naturalize) sexual subjectivities. In two justly famous interventions, *Gender Trouble: Feminism and the Subversion of Identity*, first published in 1990, and her essay "Imitation and Gender Insubordination" (1991), Butler points to performance as the site for the replication and possible contestation of both gender and sexual norms. If identity is constituted in its most mundane fashion by repetitions of behaviors and modes of self-presentation, then that repetition offers a place to locate and instigate change:

> if heterosexuality is compelled to *repeat itself* in order to establish the illusion of its own uniformity and identity, then this is an identity permanently at risk, for what if it fails to repeat, or if the very exercise of repetition is redeployed for a very different performative purpose? If there is, as it were, always a compulsion to repeat, repetition never fully accomplishes identity. That there is a need for a repetition at all is a sign that identity is not self-identical. It requires to be instituted again and again, which is to say that it runs the risk of becoming *de*-instituted at every interval.
>
> (Butler 1991: 24)

And in line with our own discussion, her primary interest is in the possibility of individual agency in achieving that *de*-institutionalization:

> The question of locating "agency" is usually associated with the viability of the "subject," where the "subject" is understood to have some stable existence prior to the cultural field that it negotiates. Or, if the subject is culturally constructed, it is nevertheless vested with an agency, usually figured as the capacity for reflexive mediation, that remains intact regardless of its cultural embeddedness. On such a model, "culture"

and "discourse" *mire* the subject, but do not constitute the subject. This move to qualify and enmire the preexisting subject has appeared necessary to establish a point of agency that is not fully *determined* by that culture and discourse. And yet, this kind of reasoning falsely presumes (a) agency can only be established through recourse to a prediscursive "I," even if that "I" is found in the midst of a discursive convergence, and (b) that to be *constituted* by discourse is to be *determined* by discourse, where determination forecloses the possibility of agency.

(Butler 1999: 182)

It is worth taking a moment to reflect on Butler's major point above. Taking social constructionism as a given, Butler argues that the repudiation of essential foundations for human subjectivity in no way precludes effective political action and subversive intervention. Simply put, constructionist theory should never be considered deterministic. While received language and categories may provide the base for resistance, they certainly do not wholly predetermine the trajectory of resistance.

In fact, Butler argues that human subjectivity is always already variable and various. Transgendered individuals, queers, and politically radical feminists already exist in defiance of the norm. Theory simply needs to catch up with, and find ways of furthering and validating, that variability. In the last famous words of *Gender Trouble*, she suggests

If identities were no longer fixed as the premises of a political syllogism, and politics no longer understood as a set of practices derived from the alleged interests that belong to a set of ready-made subjects, a new configuration of politics would surely emerge from the ruins of the old. Cultural configurations of sex and gender might then proliferate or, rather, their present proliferation might then become articulable within the discourses that establish intelligible cultural life, confounding the very binarism of sex, and exposing its fundamental unnaturalness.

(Butler 1999: 189–90)

While Butler later qualified the implicit optimism and call to activism of the statements above, her early work certainly helped propel the energetic theorizations of sexual subjectivity and identity politics of the last decade of the twentieth century.

In the words of Sue-Ellen Case, one of the first critics to use the term "queer theory," "In contrast to the gender-based construction of the lesbian in representation, queer theory, as I will construct it here, works not at the site of gender, but at the site of ontology, to shift the ground of being itself" (Case 1991: 3). That focus on ontology takes us into difficult and murky terrain, of course. Indeed, sexuality and desire are so shifting, internally complicated, and even at times ephemeral, that grounding a discussion of a continuing identity thereon is problematic to say the least, but therein also lie significant opportunities. In discussing gender we have, of course, the biological functions and contours of the human body as our points of reference, though certainly those are ascribed meaning variously and by way of shifting cultural constructs. In discussing sexuality, however, we are even farther removed from the tangible and knowable, having vectors of desire that are only imprecisely describable, and then only when we exclude the vast manifestations of fleeting and unarticulated/unarticulatable desires that we tacitly agree to ignore.

As a very simple example, "I am a heterosexual woman" or "I am a gay man" are identity statements that obscure the fact that an individual's heterosexuality or homosexuality may involve only a relatively few individuals of the "opposite" or "same" sex, considering the various complications of age and physical appearance that often render the great majority of individuals undesirable to any given person. Indeed, we might think of such statements as being predicated always on the isolation of what is *necessary* but never *sufficient* in the biology of the "desired." Obviously, there may be many other *necessaries* that we simply fail to recognize as the means for constructing sexual identity categories today, such as body size, personal hygiene, or facial features. These may or may not override, even as they complicate, biological difference as the basis for desire. But even in simply complicating slightly our notion that "heterosexuality" and "homosexuality" are perfectly sufficient categories, we are certainly encouraged to ask if there are other structuring mechanisms theorizable or circulating already that further undermine their sanctity as real and true identity categories. S&M enthusiasts, fetishists, bisexuals, and others whose desires might exceed that binary would say "yes," that sexual subjectivities are already rethinkable in ways that do not reference only and automatically genitally based differences. For Deleuze and Guattari, too, we are all filled by "desire that does not take as its object persons or things, but the entire surroundings that it traverses" (1983: 292), even if our discourse limits our ability to discuss that desire. Queer theory, as brash and iconoclastic as it can be, can still fail sometimes to deal with such complexities, as I have argued at length elsewhere (Hall 2003: 86–108). However, some of the most interesting philosophical inquiries into sexual subjectivity during the twenty-first century will certainly confront that failure as they continue to explore agency in processes of self-identification, however compromised that agency may be. If, as theorist Eve Sedgwick suggests, "'queer' can signify only *when attached to the first person*" (Sedgwick 1993: 9), the proliferation of many and imaginative possibilities for first-person sexual significations is one avenue for the deployment of power in processes of social change. Speaking out, or coming out, about different sexual desires and subjectivities is thus potentially highly dynamic because it helps expose the gross oversimplifications that underlie theories of sexual normality lingering still from the nineteenth century. If socially responsible and ethical citizens reveal unclassifiable, aberrant, and queer sexual desires, what might that tell us about the failures and potentials of received language and of theory itself to account for such complexity?

Yet however optimistic we may be about differing valuations and identifications in the future, oppression on the basis of biological sex and sexual identity is still all too common in Anglo-American society today; feminist and queer theories, even in their present form, continue to offer important opportunities for intellectually inventive and politically dynamic analysis. Indeed, it is useful to muse briefly on the differing possibilities for feminist and queer work provided even by a single text: the director Ang Lee's 1993 film *The Wedding Banquet*. This film makes some powerful statements concerning the myriad of social forces demanding conformity to traditional notions of both sexual and gender identity. The unlikely romantic triangle at its center is that of a mixed race gay couple, Wai-Tung and Simon, who live in New York, and Wai-Tung's female tenant, Wei-Wei, an artist originally from mainland China.

As Belsey might note, subjectivity is clearly displaced here across a wide range of discourses.

From a queer theoretical stance, the film certainly works to pluralize and complicate our notion of sexual identity. Simon's parents know about and accept his gay identity, but the tension of the film comes from the fact that the closeted Wai-Tung is under intense pressure from his parents, living in Taiwan, to marry and produce a child. Though the socially pervasive force of homophobia is apparent from the film's beginning, with its highlighting of the critical stares of the gay couple's neighbors, sexual subjectivity here is thoroughly complicated by ethnic and familial identity bases, challenging the audience's notion of *a* single, unified gay identity. Simon cannot understand why Wai-Tung won't "just tell them" – come out to his parents – and is mystified about why Wai-Tung participates in the charade of a singles-club marriage search that is initiated by his parents. To all of Simon's inquiries and chastisements, Wai-Tung answers with a muffled "humph"; Simon cannot understand the complexity of Wai-Tung's subject position because Simon is not a Chinese son.

The consequences of Simon's mistaken assumptions concerning what is "best" for them is clear in the havoc he creates in all of the characters' lives with the seemingly bright idea of a marriage of convenience to Wei-Wei, who desperately needs a husband for immigration purposes. The ensuing social pressures of the wedding celebration and its various traditions emphasizing reproduction, as well as the incessant demands of Wai-Tung's parents concerning the need to produce an heir, lead to a drunken sexual encounter between Wei-Wei and Wai-Tung, and an unexpected pregnancy. Certainly the film works to resolve these complications in its own queer fashion. At its conclusion, all three will raise the child in a new and different configuration of "family," and though most of the main characters, including the meddling parents, are teary-eyed and depressed in its final scene, they all have managed to survive the destructive force of familial expectations, heterosexism, and cultural tradition. *The Wedding Banquet* demonstrates that subjectivity is imbricated within a wide variety of powerful cultural forces, but in the various "outings" and revelations at the end of the film, compromised agency is still shown to be possible. Indeed, late in the film, the AIDS activist slogan "Silence=Death" is shown on a prominently displayed poster; while breaking silence on one's sexual identity (as Wai-Tung finally does with his mother) does not lead to freedom or liberation, it does represent an act of agency that in the film, as well as in Foucault's work, allows for a deployment of always compromised power.

These compromises are not limited to sexuality, for the film also conveys some powerful messages about gender and subjectivity. Wei-Wei is a complex character, who at the beginning of the film lives a bohemian lifestyle, drinking and exuberantly painting avant-garde art. But the material reality of her life is that she is a poor illegal immigrant, and if she does not marry, she will be arrested and deported. We see her experience the increasingly intense force of gendered social scripting as the preparation for the wedding banquet includes hours of application of make-up and feminine costuming. She is slowly transformed from a bohemian artist into the image of a proper Chinese bride. Yet, at the same time, Wei-Wei is not without agency; having long been attracted physically to Wai-Tung, she is the sexual aggressor who initiates their consummation, which causes her pregnancy. She is also the one who decides to keep the child. Her tradition-bound mother-in-law, who is also a powerful and complex character, admits that she envies Wei-Wei and other young women: "Independent, well-educated, with your own life. You don't depend on men. You do as you please." But of course the reality of the situation is much more complicated than that. Wei-Wei only exercises agency within the context of continuing gender expectations, as well as the realities of economics and tradition. She is shown near the end of the film painting vigorously, certainly still exercising some independence and determination, but also living a life newly entangled in social scripts of motherhood and a domestic partnership with two men. In the film's final image, the distraught parents (who are still caught up in a myriad of lies to each other and their extended family) are ready to board a plane to return to Taiwan, but must first pass through a security screening. In its frozen, emphatic image of that screening, the film captures the control, order, and regimentation that continue to impact upon, if never wholly control, all of the lives revealed in the film. No one is "free" here; all act within networks of social power that can be altered and interrogated but never simply ignored or repudiated.

RACE AND POSTCOLONIALITY

Most current discussions of subjectivity focus on the multiplicity of our social roles and identity positions. While nineteenth- and early twentieth-century expressions of identity politics often separated out a single defining characteristic as a point of powerful and practical emphasis, late twentieth-century theorizations of subjectivity often brought to the foreground complications and plural social engagements. In some ways, this intellectual sophistication can be traced back to the works of W. E. B. Du Bois and the other early theorists of race whom we discussed previously, and whose attention to class oppression clearly enriched their understanding of the challenges faced by many African-Americans. More recently, the continuing experience of gender oppression has given a particular urgency to the voices of African-American feminists, who have led the call for the recognition of *subjectivities* within disenfranchised communities.

Two of the most influential and urgent commentators during the late twentieth century on convergences and divergences in ideologies of race, class, and gender were Audre Lorde and bell hooks. In *Sister Outsider*, Lorde argues memorably:

> those of us who are poor, who are lesbians, who are Black, who are older – know that *survival is not an academic skill*. It is learning how to stand alone, unpopular and reviled, and how to make common cause with those others identified as outside the structures in order to define and seek a world in which we can all flourish. It is learning how to take our differences and make them strengths. *For the master's tools will never dismantle the master's house.*

> (Lorde 1984: 112)

Lorde thus highlights the inevitable and continuing coexistence of difference *and* commonality among groups of people, arguing for a consciousness of multiplicity in which we choose alliances but do not erase or forget distinctions. In her italicized final injunction, she evokes folk wisdom from the years of slavery to make her point that inherited language, categories, and definitions (or *discourse*, as Foucault might term it) must be interrogated if oppressed groups ever hope to challenge the status quo. And indeed, the concept that must be interrogated and repudiated most aggressively is that of one-dimensional identity as a political necessity; she sums up,

> As a Black lesbian feminist comfortable with the many different ingredients of my identity, and a woman committed to racial and sexual freedom from oppression, I find I am constantly being encouraged to pluck out some aspect of myself and present this as the meaningful whole, eclipsing or denying the other parts of my self. But this is a destructive and fragmenting way to live.
>
> (120)

Linda Garber, in her study *Identity Poetics: Race, Class, and the Lesbian-Feminist Roots of Queer Theory*, argues that Lorde's "insistence on her 'multiple selves' – her many public declarations and poetic expressions" (Garber 2001: 98) were foundational to later "queer" and other social constructionist theories, while also serving as a direct challenge to the racism and sexism of the 1970s and 1980s. Responsible agency, in Lorde's opinion, is never derived simply from acting out of one aspect of social identity, rather it comes from an awareness of the unique combinations of identities lived and experienced by the individual, whose power to respond to oppression thus originates in a critical consciousness of being athwart several, even numerous, social categories.

bell hooks makes a similar theoretical point in her influential essay "Postmodern Blackness," where she argues that "Employing a critique of essentialism . . . allows us to affirm multiple black identities, varied black experience. It also challenges colonial imperialist paradigms of black identity which represent blackness one-dimensionally in ways that reinforce and sustain white supremacy" (hooks 1994: 425). She too urges for a recognition of "multiple experiences of black identity that are the lived conditions which make diverse cultural productions possible" (426). And out of that awareness can come political agency:

> Postmodern culture with its decentered subject can be the space where ties are severed or it can provide the occasion for new and varied forms of bonding. To some extent, ruptures, surfaces, contextuality, and a host of other happenings create gaps that make space for oppositional

> practices which no longer require intellectuals to be confined by narrow
> separate spheres with no meaningful connection to the world of the
> everyday.
>
> (427)

For hooks and many other recent theorists of race, late twentieth-century, postmodern perspectives on subjectivity can usefully erase the boundaries of high and low culture, challenge essentialist divisions among peoples, and complicate racial identity with an awareness of differences of gender, class, and sexuality within communities in ways that are politically dynamic. In hooks's opinion that dynamism must begin with "critical dialogue" between black "writers and scholars" and the "black underclass," among many other groups; indeed, such "exchange . . . may very well be 'the' central future location of resistance struggle" (427). hooks thereby offers a model of dialogism that constitutes a decisive "critical break with the notion of 'authority' as 'mastery over'" (423). The notion of the decentered subject here decenters even the subjectivity of the commentator on subjectivity.

These insights are some of the most exciting in current discussions of subjectivity generally. Mae Gwendolyn Henderson speaks specifically to black women's subjectivity, but with implications for the entire field of subjectivity studies, when she writes of "the plural aspects of self that constitute the matrix of black female subjectivity. The interlocutory character of black women's writings is, thus, not only a consequence of a dialogic relationship with an imaginary or 'generalized Other,' but a dialogue with the aspects of 'otherness' within the self" (Henderson 1994: 258–59). Such always inherent multiplicity is explored also by Gloria Anzaldúa in her work on *mestiza* subjectivity. In *Borderlands/ La Frontera* (1999) she echoes other theorists in recognizing that subjectivities are formed in and through language. But theorizing from her own position as a Chicana, growing up in a Spanish-speaking community within a larger English-speaking context, she focuses on the hybrid, metamorphic nature of subjectivities on the borderlands of linguistic conflict and accommodation.

> For a people who are neither Spanish nor live in a country in which
> Spanish is the first language; for a people who live in a country in which

English is the reigning tongue but who are not Anglo; for a people who cannot entirely identify with either the standard (formal, Castilian) Spanish nor standard English, what recourse is left to them but to create their own language? . . . . We speak a patois, a forked tongue, a variation of two languages.

(Anzaldúa 1999: 77)

Furthermore, as a woman and a self-identified "queer," she continues to complicate and recomplicate the identities that demand individualized negotiation and decision-making: "I *made the choice to be queer*" (41). The agency that is derived from the recognition of in-betweenness, of a forthright "struggle of identities," a "struggle of borders" (85), is both specific to Anzaldúa's own subject position(s) and challenging to all of us who live multiply, variously, and in differing ways in-between and among identity bases. Indeed, her work urges us to recognize that there is a point of significant agency involved always in a fundamental decision we must make over whether subjectivity is reduced to being singular or *allowed to be* multiple, and further agency/choice involved in what a recognition of multiplicity then allows in terms of creating affiliation with others whose subjectivities are similarly complicated and multiple. Subjectivity may never be under any firm or even measurable degree of control, however, *what we do with our understanding of subjectivity* is clearly susceptible to some degree of control.

This notion of agency raises the question of whether or not there is ever a point of such dire abjection or debasement that subjectivity itself is wholly imperceptible and unknowable by the theorist or commentator. Gayatri Spivak explores this issue in one of the foundational texts of postcolonial studies: "Can the Subaltern Speak?" Postcolonial studies have taken the discussion of tendentious categories of race and ethnicity and explored how such classifications have led to terrible forms of exploitation among nations and regions of the world, and indeed, how subjectivity itself has been colonized. In "Can the Subaltern Speak?" Spivak notes that any attempt to recover the voices, perspectives, and subjectivities of the socially outcast and illiterate is heavily compromised if not doomed: "When we come to the concomitant question of the consciousness of the subaltern, the notion of what the work *cannot* say becomes important. . . . The sender – 'the peasant' – is marked only as a pointer to an irretrievable consciousness" (Spivak 1988: 287). She goes on to argue even more urgently that within "the effaced itinerary of the subaltern subject . . . the subaltern as female is even more deeply in shadow" (287). When postcolonial theorists speak of the "Hindu widow [who] ascends the pyre of the dead husband and immolates herself upon it . . . [one] never encounters the testimony of the women's voice-consciousness" (297). Indeed, in the texts such as police reports that describe these acts, "one cannot put together a 'voice'," only "an immense heterogeneity" (297). Of course, in interacting critically with such cases, one is not left without markers of something like agency; after all, sporadic peasant insurgency and even self-immolation could be *theorized* as such, but what is missing wholly is any trace of voiced self-expression. In making this point, Spivak's work is not intended to silence the cultural critic, but it does foreground the impositions and reconstructions of voice that always attend and complicate postcolonial studies. As Ania Loomba sums up,

> Spivak's point . . . [is to] challenge the easy assumption that the postcolonial historian can recover the standpoint of the subaltern. At the same time, she takes seriously the desire, on the part of postcolonial intellectuals, to highlight oppression and to provide the perspective of oppressed people. . . . She effectively warns the postcolonial critic against romanticizing and homogenizing the subaltern subject.
>
> (Loomba 1998: 234–35)

As was the case with Lorde, hooks, and Anzaldúa, Spivak thus complicates usefully our convenient but reductive analytical categories: she "challenges a simple division between colonizers and colonized by inserting the 'brown woman' as a category oppressed by both" (Loomba 1998: 234). Here as before, the privileged theorist's always-compromised authority should never be acted out as mastery. And this is one of the most important insights offered by postcolonial critics for subjectivity studies today: that real human consciousnesses and self-identities do not fall into the neat, polarized categories used commonly in the analysis of oppression.

Frantz Fanon and Homi Bhabha are key theorists of the colonized consciousness, the subjectivity of the individual within a culturally, linguistically, and economically occupied nation or region whose self-hood is a site both of occupation and response. Fanon's *Black Skin, White Masks*, first published in French in 1952, is a powerful reading of the "inferiority complex" (Fanon 1967: 18) created in the colonial subject; Fanon calls for "an effort at disalienation" (231) that is primarily an act of continuing analysis and inter-personal contact: "to scrutinize the self . . . to touch the other, to feel the other, to explain the other to myself" (231). As Loomba notes, Fanon's work was "explosive" because it challenged contemporary racist theories which "suggested that colonialism was the *result* of certain psychic differences between races (which lead some people to dependency or the need to be ruled)" arguing instead that "colonialism was the *cause* which engendered psychic difference along racial lines and annihilated the black subject into nothingness" (Loomba 1998: 143).

A generation later, Homi Bhabha applauded Fanon as "the purveyor of the transgressive and transitional truth" (Bhabha 1994: 40), yet Bhabha moves in a different, Foucauldian direction, after terming Fanon's conclusion to touch and feel, as quoted above, "as banal as it is beatific" (61). Bhabha argues that it is "possible . . . to redeem the pathos of cultural confusion into a strategy of political subversion" (62), one in which "ambivalent identification" or self-conscious masking, is used "audaciously to announce the important artifice of cultural identity and its difference" (63–64). He argues that "mimicry, hybridity, sly civility . . . this liminal moment of identification – eluding resemblance – produces a subversive strategy of subaltern agency that negotiates its own authority" (185). This form of agency "requires direction and contingent closure but no teleology and holism . . . because the agent . . . is in the dialogic position of calculation, negotiation, interrogation" (185). Bhabha repudiates essentialist foundations as he argues not against the material reality of oppression, of course, but rather for a supple awareness of diverse manifestations of agency and a range of subjectivities within artificially homogenized groups of oppressed peoples, who must adopt varying tactics that will allow them to survive, even in individualized ways, thrive, on day-to-day bases. Bhabha urges us to see the adoption of a mask or sly role as an instance of performative agency that unsettles, effects change, and ironizes all notions of *real* identity.

This desire to complicate racial and postcolonial subject positions through an insistence on gender, class, and sexual differences, as well as a recognition of the hybrid nature of lives lived in global interminglings of culture, language, and value, is clear in the recent writings of the Antiguan writer Jamaica Kincaid. Kincaid never dismisses contextual oppression but she is also unwilling to homogenize artificially subject positions in postcolonial spaces. The autobiographical narrative *My Brother* offers some useful examples. In it Kincaid records her actions leading up to and then thoughts following the death of her youngest brother from AIDS. While she and Devon share a cultural and familial background, Kincaid struggles to come to any understanding of Devon's motivations and degree of self-awareness; she fails finally even to make sense of his day-to-day activities. Both were similarly oppressed by a controlling and sometimes destructive mother and also by a shared experience of class deprivation and marginalized existence in the postcolonial Caribbean, but while Kincaid, who is burdened with the additional weight of debilitating gender norms and expectations, chooses escape and creative expression, Devon sinks into alcohol and drug use, petty crime, and other self-destructive activities. One piece, among many that are missing, of the puzzle of his life is the revelation after his death of Devon's occasional sexual activity with other men, and his participation in a secretive support network in Antigua for bisexuals and homosexuals. Yet even that aspect of his identity hardly *explains* Devon or his choices in any definitive way.

Perhaps most pertinent to our discussion here is Kincaid's profound interest in the question of agency and the extent to which one finally holds another person responsible for his or her life: "I looked at my brother . . . and I wondered, if his life had taken a certain turn, if he had caused his life to take a different turn, might he have written a book . . . ?" (Kincaid 1997: 11). That sentence's vacillation between the passive and active voices encapsulates the struggle that Kincaid engages in to understand the intersection of subjectivity and responsibility. Devon is a cipher: "Nothing came from him; not work, not children, not love for someone else" (13). Certainly Kincaid can catalogue her brother's abilities, his dreams of being a singer, his physical qualities and complex interactions with their mother, with whom he lives until his death, yet still she cannot understand him or why he continues to engage in self-destructive activity, including unsafe sex, even after his diagnosis with AIDS.

Locked up inside him was someone who would have spoken to the world in an important way. I believe this. Locked up inside him was someone who would have found satisfaction speaking to the world in an important way. . . . But he was not even remotely aware of such a person inside him. It was I who told him this and he agreed with me at the moment I told him this, and he said yes, and I saw that he wished what I said were really true, would just become true, wished he could, wished he knew how to make the effort and make it true.

(59–60)

"Who is he? I kept asking myself. Who is he?" (69). She does not know. Devon dies "without ever understanding or knowing, or being able to let the world in which he lived know, who he was; that who he really was – not a single sense of identity but all the complexities of who he was – he could not express fully" (162). And it is that last implication that is perhaps the most important, for one can, as Kincaid does, at the very least *attempt* to express one's complexities, even if one inevitably fails. But her brother did not or could not even make the attempt.

Indeed, that opacity of inner being, that murky line between *inability* and *unwillingness* to take responsibility and at least to attempt to become an agent, whatever one's circumstances of race, gender, sexuality, and familial relationship, will always be the limit point of any discussion of subjectivity, however authoritatively its theoreticians may present their cases.

4

POSTMODERNISM AND THE QUESTION OF AGENCY

HARAWAY AND CYBORG SUBJECTIVITY

Subjectivity, once considered potentially knowable and conceptually one-dimensional, has been rendered various, fractured, and indefinite in recent theorizations, largely because of a new recognition of the complexity of our social roles and the multiplicity of our interactions. However, in the past two decades especially, science and technology have even more dramatically complicated the ongoing discussion of who we are and the extent to which we have agency over the many aspects of our selves. Indeed, given new technologies that allow us to change our physical bodies and augment our abilities in sometimes subtle, sometimes spectacular ways, "what is *the* self?" and even "what is *a* self?" are questions that are ever more difficult to answer.

Philosopher of consciousness John Searle has asked some particularly intriguing questions about the implications of the interfacing of technology and human selfhood. In *The Rediscovery of the Mind*, he muses on the limits of consciousness and conscious intent by speculating on what might happen if an individual's brain were gradually altered through the introduction of increasing numbers of silicon chips. His *gedanken-experiment* lays out three possibilities: first, that the subject's external behaviors and consciousness might remain wholly unaltered; second, that the subject's behaviors might remain the same but consciousness of selfhood might gradually disappear; and finally, that the subject's consciousness might remain the same but external actions gradually cease. His major point is that consciousness, or subjectivity, should always be considered conceptually distinct from external behavior; he reiterates this point with another hypothetical case in which fully conscious, highly skilled robots are given the task of creating copies of themselves with exactly the same skills but with no consciousness. The result would be entities whose external behaviors are precisely the same, but in which consciousness is lacking. Searle thereby argues that we can never observe external behavior and render definitive judgments about consciousness. Searle even questions explicitly all quick ascriptions of "intent," arguing that external behaviors do not derive necessarily from intent nor does conscious intent lead necessarily or directly to behavior (Searle 1994: 65–71). These theoretical musings and hypothetical complications have a real-life importance today as we grapple with the consequences of the many new interfaces between human consciousness and technology, including pharmacology. If one is legitimately prescribed a drug that unexpectedly causes violent, even murderous, behavior, who, if anyone, is responsible for that violence? Where does subjectivity begin and end in our era of mind-altering pharmaceuticals?

Questions concerning the increasingly murky boundaries of selfhood have been asked also by Deleuze and Guattari in both *Anti-Oedipus* (1983) and in *A Thousand Plateaus* (1987). In the latter work they suggest that our era is one in which humans no longer "use" machines in traditional ways:

> cybernetic and informational machines form a [new] age that reconstructs a generalized regime of subjection: recurrent and reversible "humans-machines systems" replace the old nonrecurrent and nonreversible relations of subjection between the two elements; the relation between human and machine is based on internal, mutual communication, and no longer on usage or action.
>
> (Deleuze and Guattari 1987: 458)

They even make a credible case that humans today might be considered "enslaved by TV . . . insofar as the television viewers are no longer consumers or users, nor even subjects who supposedly 'make' it, but intrinsic component pieces" or "constituent parts" of a broader system of "input" and "output," one of "transformations and exchanges of information" (458). In drawing out the full implications of Deleuze and Guattari's work, Brian Massumi claims that:

> there is no [longer any] self-sufficient agency that can qualify as intentional. There are varying degrees of choice at successive threshold states. The "will" to change or stay the same is not an act of determination on the part of a unified subject in simple response to self-reflection or an internal impulse. It is a state of self-organized indeterminacy in response to complex causal constraints. It constitutes a real degree of freedom, but the choice belongs to the overall dissipative system with its plurality of selves, and not to the person; it is objectively co-caused at the crossroads of chance and determinacy.
>
> (Massumi 1992: 81)

For traditionalists, this self-organized indeterminacy might be terrifying, but for others, it represents a clear opportunity to rethink what we mean by subjectivity and agency in a postmodern, technology-dependent world, one far removed from that of Descartes and his self-assured *cogito*.

The scientist and cultural critic Donna Haraway has been one of the most vocal proponents of using this ongoing, deepening interfacing of humans and technology as the occasion to rethink subjectivity in radical, but at the same time, *ethically responsible* ways. Her most famous piece, reprinted numerous times after its first publication in 1985, is "A Cyborg Manifesto," which also appears as a chapter in her influential book *Simians, Cyborgs, and Women: The Reinvention of Nature* (1991). In it she argues that in "the late twentieth century, our time, a mythic time, we are all chimeras, theorized and fabricated hybrids of machine and organism; in short, we are cyborgs. The cyborg is our ontology; it gives us our politics" (Haraway 1991: 150). In stating this, Haraway is highlighting the many ways that our lives and consciousnesses depend upon, and mesh ontologically with, a variety of nonhuman entities, including computers, television, artificial limbs and organs, and controlled living environments.

Our politics already derive subtly but inevitably from this meshing; Haraway argues that we must be more forthright in discussing, confronting, and living responsibly with this imbrication.

Haraway, therefore, has no patience with anti-technology diatribes, which she considers naive and even inherently dishonest; from its opening paragraphs hers is "an argument for *pleasure* in the confusion of boundaries and for *responsibility* in their construction" (150).

> From one perspective, a cyborg world is about the final imposition of a grid of control on the planet. . . . From another perspective, a cyborg world might be about lived social and bodily realities in which people are not afraid of their joint kinship with animals and machines, not afraid of permanently partial identities and contradictory standpoints. The political struggle is to see from both perspectives at once because each reveals both dominations and possibilities unimaginable from the other vantage point. Single vision produces worse illusions than double vision or many-headed monsters.
>
> (154)

Thus one of Haraway's most important contributions to theories of subjectivity is her call for a self-conscious embracing of "permanent partiality" (173). She sums up her main points in her last paragraph:

> first, the production of universal, totalizing theory is a major mistake that misses most of reality, probably always, but certainly now; and second, taking responsibility for the social relations of science and technology means refusing an anti-science metaphysics, a demonology of technology, and so means embracing the skilful task of reconstructing the boundaries of daily life, in partial connection with others, in communication with all of our parts. . . . This is a dream not of a common language, but of a powerful infidel heteroglossia.
>
> (181)

Haraway asks us to grapple with the often-ignored complexity of our mundane existence and in ways that place responsibility and ethical choice at the center of our discussions of postmodern subjectivity. In the passage above, she calls for *skillfulness* in the deployment of agency over our own lives and interfacings, but implicitly rejects as delusional any notion of *mastery* in that deployment. In effect, she asks us *to do the best we can*, given our own partiality and limitations, but always to approach the complexity of contemporary life as directly and with as much honesty as possible.

As Christina Crosby has argued, "One of the great virtues of Donna Haraway's work . . . is that the subject is at first unrecognizable" (Crosby 1992: 138). Haraway's conception of subjectivity, Crosby suggests, "is not founded on a standpoint which in turn depends on an ontology, but on shifting, mobile, simultaneous, multiple positions, critical positions which are taken up in response to domination. That is, political positions" (139). Indeed, these are the qualities and movements in relationship to individual experience and selfhood that commonly define postmodern existence as a late twentieth-century and now twenty-first-century phenomenon. Certainly the numerous works that acknowledge and expand upon Haraway's work reiterate this point often. Chris Gray argues in *Cyborg Citizen*, "*Meanings are constructed*, which means they can be chosen. . . . We are involved in participatory evolution, and that means the responsibility to participate is ours" (Gray 2001: 199). And even those theorists who offer the most incisive rejoinders to Haraway, from postcolonial perspectives, for example, do not dismiss the first-world ubiquity and worldwide effect of cyborgism and that notion of participatory evolution, even if participation in it is limited to a privileged few: "The cyborg is not the general, postmodern form of subjectivity created by multinational capitalism but rather the hegemonic subject position that its ideology privileges" (Gabilondo 1995: 424). Joseba Gabilondo goes on to assert, "Postcolonial subjectivity has to be understood as the interface of precolonial, colonial, and mass-culture logics" (430). While he rejects the term "cyborg" as an accurate descriptor of subjectivity in the so-called "Third World," where pervasive technology is hardly a fact of life, Gabilondo does argue that "From the cyborg to the Third World consumer 'Man' and the postcolonial subaltern," any "cultural politics that does not account for the new interfacial positions of all these cultural parameters [will] block any possibility for progressive politics" (430–31). Agency in the cause of progressive politics thus depends upon an active grappling with partiality, technological interfacing, and hybridization. According to Gabilondo, any theorist still positing the ideal of wholly rational self-reflection and quasi-Cartesian self-knowledge achievement is resorting to facile utopianism and a potentially disastrous form of willful blindness.

Science fiction writers have long mused on the political implications of such complex interfacings of humans and technology. Over a century ago, H. G. Wells's *The Island of Dr. Moreau* (1896) offered stern warnings concerning the ability of science to blur the boundaries of the human and nonhuman. Ridley Scott's film *Blade Runner* (1982) is perhaps the most famous recent meditation on the technologically complicated, and ever more emotionally and politically charged, boundaries of subjectivity. Its plot concerns the attempt by a police officer, Deckard (played by Harrison Ford), to track down and kill a small group of rebel robots, or "replicants," who are practically indistinguishable from human beings. As he violently "retires," or from another perspective, murders, the replicants, Deckard and the film begin to grapple with the question of who/what is human or close enough to being human to be worthy of respect and life. Led by Roy, the rebels have returned to earth in a desperate attempt to find a way of prolonging their life span beyond a 4-year self-destruct mechanism. After first positioning the replicants as simple action-drama villains, the film slowly and masterfully reveals the intense anguish of these near-humans who, we learn, simply wish to be allowed to live. Indeed, we discover that the only known difference between humans and replicants is that the latter are supposedly unable to empathize, a distinction which is so subtle that it is only revealed through prolonged testing of a suspicious individual. And even that sole, supposed difference is wholly discredited at the end of the film, when it is Roy who empathizes and saves Deckard's life, even though the humans are consistently unable to empathize with the replicants and their anguished situation.

The replicant Pris asks one of her still skeptical makers for his respect and his recognition of her basic right to exist by asserting the well-known Cartesian formula: "I think, Sebastian, therefore I am." The *cogito* retains a certain conceptual weight and validity here, not because of any lingering credibility ascribed to the ideal of self-assured knowledge, but rather because it forces us to confront the issue of political rights. The film demonstrates that the replicants have subjectivities that are as highly developed and intensely personal as any human being, even if they are technologically created. The fact that some of their memories may be implanted does not render their experience of the world and their emotional relationships any less real or poignant. As Roy dies his pre-programmed death, he tries to make Deckard understand: "I've seen things you people wouldn't believe. . . . All those moments will be lost in time like tears in the rain." He is condemned to death simply because he is categorized as subhuman, which gives the film a powerful political subtext. Just before he generously saves Deckard's life, even as he loses his own, Roy comments, "Quite an experience to live in fear, isn't it? That's what it is to be a slave." Roy's statement links the question of the humanity of robots with a long history of identity political struggles over categories of beings excluded from basic human rights. Scott's film, through the medium of science fiction, poses thereby a potent philo-sophical question: "Who or what possesses subjectivity?" Simply put, who *is* a *who* rather than a *what*? In directly engaging that issue, the film challenges us to ponder not only questions of technological innovation and creation, but even ongoing struggles over issues such as animal rights. Are gorillas painting pictures and communicating in sign language a "who"? Are dolphins speaking to each other in high-pitched tones and greeting humans with curiosity a "who"? No doubt, these will be ever more contested questions as genetic manipulations and the possi-bilities of cloning lead to even more blurred boundaries between the "who" and the "what." Haraway argues that cyborgism *will* give us our politics in increasingly complicated and emotionally charged ways. Postmodern agency begins at the meta-theoretical level with a recognition and forthright admission of that fact.

SUBJECTIVITIES

Indeed, that question of agency remains at the heart of discussions of subjectivity today. And this is not simply an academic, abstract, and impractical question. It is, in small and large ways, a matter of life and death. That fact is one that I hope all readers of the present book will remember long after they finish these concluding paragraphs. "Agency," its possibility and practicality, brings us face to face with the political question of how we can motivate ourselves and others to work for social change and economic justice; that *does* mean life and death for vast numbers of people living in poverty, inhabiting countries branded simplistically as "evil," and living with grave illnesses, including breast cancer and AIDS. Do we respond to injustice and the Machiavellian moves of politicians and business leaders with cynicism or with a belief that human beings, individually and collectively, can change for the better, if they revisit some fundamental decisions about their own priorities and values?

In broader ways, the question of agency, and our ability to act with intent and awareness, raises also the question of how we conceive of and define responsibility and culpability. It is all well and good to proclaim, as Judith Butler does in *Bodies that Matter*, that "the subject as a self-identical entity is no more" (Butler 1993: 230), but when that conflicted, inchoate, non-self-identical entity is gay-bashing, raping, or carving a swastika into someone, even the most postmodern of theorists would want the subject in question to be held, in some form or fashion, responsible for his or her actions. These are some of the most difficult issues facing us today. To what extent and how do we hold the impoverished, urban teenaged boy, steeped in cultural beliefs involving machismo and church-supported homophobia, responsible for his violent actions? And as legislators in the United States debate laws allowing the execution even of minors and the mentally impaired, the thoughtful, careful ascription of intent and responsibility is one of *clear* life-and-death urgency.

The fact that there are no final and definitive answers to such questions should be the spur to continuing analytical work and ongoing critical dialogue; it should never serve as an excuse for cynicism or, worse yet, an invitation to resort to some outdated, discredited paradigm from years or centuries past. Certainly the latter is the easy route taken by too many groups and politicians, with the resurgence we have seen in religious fundamentalism, dogmatism, and law-and-order conservatism. Whether from the right (most often) or the left (occasionally), these are efforts to end discussion through formulae and obstinate adherence to failed templates that offer quick comfort in their simplicity.

Indeed, discussion and dialogue, attended always by an acknowledgment of complexity and commitment to critical reflection, remain key to the work on subjectivity. It is useful to hear the relative optimism expressed by Lawrence M. Friedman that today "one even chooses (within limits) a race, a gender, a form of sexuality" (Friedman 1999: 240); at the same time we do recognize that one's choices are always highly circum-scribed and that in theorizing wide-ranging, self-aware "choice" one also raises the issue of *responsibility* for choosing carefully throughout one's life and activities. It is likewise useful to hear sociologist Anthony Giddens hold out great hope for the "everyday social experiments" (Giddens 1992: 8) in which many people engage today with increasing fervor. Giddens, in books such as *The Consequences of Modernity* (1990), *Modernity and Self-Identity* (1991), and *The Transformation of Intimacy* (1992), constructs a revisionary sociology of self-aware agency that does not posit perfectly achievable states of self-knowledge, but does suggest an ability today to experiment with and choose among possible lifestyles, modes of self-presentation, and affiliations, abetted by new technologies and increased flows of information through the Web and media. Needless to say, such celebrations of first-world, privileged-class eclecticism say little about the choices available to the poor and those displaced by war and famine. And even within the circumscribed geography of the first world, we still must complicate any designation of possible agency with an awareness of greatly varied material resources and education levels, degrees of gender and racial privilege, comfort levels with technology, and even mental health and all of the myriad of other factors that can affect one's ability to choose carefully, take risks bravely, and accept failure or criticism without paralysis or other self-destructive response. As Stjepan Mestrovic, one of Giddens's most fervent critics, notes, "human agents do create knowledgeable and meaningful repre-sentations of the world in their quest for what might be termed agency, as Giddens maintains, but they are also driven by powerful and often hidden and mysterious passions, something that Giddens never acknowledges" (Mestrovic 1998: 49–50).

This need to accompany optimism over agency with a recognition of the many psychic forces that will always exceed human control is the thrust of Judith Butler's refinements of her early 1990s work on subjectivity and performative agency. Her emphasis in *Gender Trouble* on the *visibly* discursive means by which our identities are manifested and maintained led to some sloppy readings, ones that misconstrued her point as one suggesting that we have unfettered agency over those identities. She retorts: "The bad reading goes something like this: I can get up in the morning, look in my closet, and decide which gender I want to be today. I can take out a piece of clothing and change my gender, stylize it, and then that evening I can change it again and be something radically other" (cit. Glover and Kaplan 2000: xxvii). As David Glover and Cora Kaplan note, this misses a key point, that "Like the everyday use of language from which it partly derives, gender underpins our capacity to make decisions and act upon them, while constantly slipping out of our control and ensnaring us in complex webs of meaning that no single individual can ever hope to master" (xxvii). We are *subject* to discourse, not simply *subjects through* discourse with the ability to turn around, contemplate, and rework our subjectivity at will.

In *The Psychic Life of Power: Theories in Subjection*, Butler highlights the difficulty of theorizing agency when one recognizes also the power of interpellation. She remains, however, cautiously optimistic: "Agency exceeds the power by which it is enabled. . . . [A]gency is the assumption of a purpose *unintended* by power" (Butler 1997: 15). At the same time, Butler also desires to make the constraints on that subversive assumption of power clear: "To claim that the subject exceeds . . . is not to claim that it lives in some free zone of its own making. Exceeding is not escaping, and the subject exceeds precisely that to which it is bound" (17). Her point is well taken, even if her lines circumscribing agency may be cautiously opened up even a bit more. In *Bodies that Matter* she notes that "Identifications are multiple and contestatory" (Butler 1993: 99), yet in *The Psychic Life of Power* Butler never fully explores the great and often highly conflicted multiplicity of interpellations that we all encounter and embody, as gendered, sexualized, racialized beings. She argues cogently that, "we might reread 'being' as precisely the potentiality that remains unexhausted by any particular interpellation. Such a failure of interpellation may well undermine the capacity of the subject to 'be' in a self-identical sense, but it may also mark the path toward a more open, even ethical, kind of being, one of or for the future" (Butler 1997: 131). We might take that insight and pluralize it, recognizing that *interpellations* fail and conflict all the time. We might then open it up further still by citing her point that if the "subject produces its coherence at the cost of its own complexity, the crossings of identification of which it is itself composed, then that subject forecloses the kinds of contestatory connections that might democratize the field of its own operation" (Butler 1993: 115); in thinking about that dynamic, we might arrive at an expanded notion of *potential* agency that approaches the optimism of Giddens without ignoring those limitations resulting inevitably from the interpellative process and the parameters of discourse itself. If the subject can choose to *foreclose* contestatory connections, then certainly it has an always limited but still significant ability to *allow* those contestatory connections, or at least to recognize their possibility.

Butler herself states that she "invest[s] no ultimate political hope in the possibility of avowing identifications that have conventionally been disavowed" (Butler 1993: 115), for "certain disavowals are fundamentally enabling, and . . . no subject can proceed, can act, without disavowing certain possibilities and avowing others" (116). However, an underlying implication of her work and the explicit point that I wish to emphasize here is that a *critical consciousness* of that dynamic is potentially, at least, highly generative of subversion and of always compromised and contextually imbricated agency. We can find it both intellectually and politically empowering to examine critically how, and to what extent, we might avow and disavow our identifications, how we are variously interpellated and enact those interpellations through our mundane activities and continuing frames of reference, and how we do exist and can change in/over time. After all, it is a simple but clear fact that change, in social norms and in valuations of gender, sexuality, race, and class, occurs inevitably, sometimes incrementally, sometimes relatively quickly. As Butler notes, "If the conditions of power are to persist, they must be reiterated; the subject is precisely the site of such reiteration, a repetition that is never merely mechanical" (Butler 1997: 16). We are not automatons, and in spite of our many and various interpellations and sometimes active, sometimes passive identificatory choices, the terms of subjectivity itself remain malleable, even if never free-floating or open to anything approaching unfettered control.

If there is a common political thrust to much contemporary critical theory, whether concerned with conditions of postcoloniality, gender, class, or sexuality, it is that subjectivity itself is textual. And that is a dynamic insight and perhaps the most important point of this book. To de-naturalize our *selves* is not to make them easily manipulable, but it is to disrupt and disturb the *automatism* of their relationship to the fixed scripts and values of the past (and the present, too, in the dogma of fundamentalism, narrow essentialism, and other reactionary movements).

In textualizing my selfhood, in opening up for critical analysis, both self-directed and communal, my own affiliations, choices, exclusions, valuations, and engagements as a queer, white, atheist, middle-class, academic American man, among other aspects of my subjectivity, I at least open up for discussion and revision the responsibility that I bring to those subject position(ing)s. This is not to posit an end-point of full ethical self-awareness, but it is to acknowledge the necessity of struggling with the issue of accountability and responsibility in an environment in which we grapple with, rather than nervously avoid, questions of human rights, class inequities, and the effects of technology on our selves and our interactions with each other and the natural world. As Zygmunt Bauman argues,

> One might say that postmodernity is an "era of morality" in one sense only: . . . it is possible now, nay inevitable, to face the moral issues point-blank, in all their naked truth, as they emerge from the life experience of men and women, and as they confront moral selves in all their irreparable and irredeemable ambivalence.
>
> Paradoxically, it is only now that actions appear to the moral selves as matters of responsible choice. . . . The denizens of the postmodern era are, so to speak, forced to stand face-to-face with their moral autonomy, and so also with their moral responsibility. This is the cause of moral agony. This is also the chance the moral selves never confronted before.
>
> (Bauman 1995: 42–43)

It is this process of confrontation and critical analysis of morality as a human construct, one tied in mundane and broadly discursive ways to our enactments of selfhood, that offers the possibility for revision of those selves and for discrete acts of political agency.

Interpellations and other processes of subject creation are numerous, always partial, often recurring and reinforced, but also potentially lapsing. Those lapses can be forced and temporary, as one might experience in the use of drugs or through music or dance, or they can be more unexpected but temporally significant, as might occur through encounters with illness or trauma, or even with significant changes in life situation or interpersonal context. But in recognizing that subjectivity is neither diachronically static nor synchronically one-dimensional, we can find in the field of subjectivity studies many opportunities for both abstract intellectual and concrete, directly political work. That dynamism can only be fueled, of course, by what is finally a creative act: that of imagining that what *is* does not necessarily *have to be*. In positing what we, *our selves*, would like to be, we challenge our selves and each other with the necessary interplay of the *real*, the mundane and restrictive, and the *ideal*, the carefully imagined and even tentatively utopian. Thus Descartes's *cogito* might be rewritten today to read: *We think . . . and rethink . . . and therefore we are*. Only by pluralizing our intellectual engagements and activities by recognizing *community* and foregrounding the necessary, ongoing revision of those engagements is human *being* rendered significantly different from the *being* of those entities that are instinct-driven or simply mechanical. And even if we blur those differentiations between human and animal, and human and machine, often and usefully, that act of complication should never be in the service of excusing our own carelessness, selfishness, or cynicism. We must never forget that even if we do not create our *selves* in any neat or instrumental way, we do collectively create the conditions of our own survival or destruction.

GLOSSARY

Cogito: in his fourth "Discourse on Method," the seventeenth-century philosopher René Descartes offers his famous principle, known as the *cogito*, "I think, therefore I am." This principle had a profound influence on later philosophy because it newly isolated *self*-awareness and reflection upon the *individual* as a thinking unit, rather than inter-relationship or broad communal processes, as the central focus of theories of human being and meaning.

Cyborg: in both science fiction and late twentieth-century cultural theory, the term cyborg is used to describe a melding of the human and the nonhuman within a single entity. A concrete example of a cyborg would be a person whose abilities are enhanced by robotics, such as portrayed in the television show "The Six Million Dollar Man" or the film *Robocop*. More broadly, theorist Donna Haraway uses the term to point to the growing inter-relationship and the increasingly murky boundaries between the human and nonhuman that we now experience in our dependence upon Web-based communication, controlled living environments, pace-makers, and even contact lenses.

Discourse: this term is used in the theories of Michel Foucault and other twentieth-century philosophers and critics to point broadly to any means by which human meanings, beliefs, and values are communicated and replicated. Language is the most obvious example of discourse. Meaning is also conveyed by clothing, gestures, images, and a wide variety of other nonverbal manifestations of discourse. Sometimes the term is used more narrowly to point out the meanings and values within a discrete area of human knowledge and activity, such as "gender discourse" or "sexual discourse."

Epistemology: this is the branch of philosophy that asks the question "How do we know what we know?" Epistemology explores the creation and classification of knowledge and the values we ascribe to it.

Essentialism: we term theories and belief systems "essentialist" when they suggest that differences between men and women, between heterosexuals and homosexuals, or among races are based in aspects of biology, metaphysical reality, or anything else outside of human cultural values or processes of meaning making. The term points to a belief in an "essence" that precedes any human thinking or activity in constructing difference (see Social constructionism below for a contrast).

Existentialism: this branch of philosophy holds as its core principle that "existence precedes essence," or in other words, that human beings came into existence through natural, evolutionary processes, and then created myths and religious beliefs to explain their uniqueness and importance. Existentialist philosophers such as Friedrich Nietzsche, Jean Paul Sartre, and Albert Camus suggested that human beings must confront their own responsibility for creating lives and values that did not depend upon the crutch of tradition and religious beliefs.

Identity politics: beginning with the feminist and anti-slavery movements of the eighteenth and nineteenth centuries, identity became politicized as groups of disenfranchised individuals came to reflect on their common experience of oppression. For the first time, the social values ascribed to one's identity became challengeable and changeable during that time period because they were newly perceived as human constructs.

Ideology: while different theorists will define this term with different emphases and inflections, common to most definitions is a reference to an underlying belief or value system that may be wholly unacknowledged or that is simply held to be *real* or natural but that orders and organizes the world in ways that has political consequences. For Karl Marx, ideology was used to describe those economic beliefs, falsely held to be naturally or divinely ordained, that unfairly privileged some individuals and kept large sectors of the population in oppressive circumstances. For others, ideology means any belief that carries political values and that deserves critical attention and challenge.

Interpellation: this term, originating in the theories of Louis Althusser and referenced by later theorists, uses a striking metaphor to capture the process by which we acquire our social identities. We are interpellated, or hailed, by ideology in the same way we might be hailed by a police officer on the street. We respond to that hailing automatically, turning around as if acknowledging our guilt, and in doing so assume a certain identity. Interpellation captures the power behind social categories and the ways that we are conscripted into our social identities, a process that the politically attuned theorist of interpellation seeks to foreground and challenge.

Ontology: this branch of philosophy concerns the nature of "being" and existence. It muses on questions such as "what is existence?" and "how does human *being* differ from that of animals and other entities?"

Postcolonial theory: this recent field of speculation in cultural theory confronts the legacy of imperialism and the long history of colonial domination of regions and groups of people. Besides exploring the economic and cultural consequences of colonialism, it also probes the psychological effects of being a member of an ethnic group or race defined and treated as inferior. It examines the ways that selfhood among the colonized was shaped by colonial value systems and the continuing impact of those value systems and responses to those value systems today.

Postmodernism and poststructuralism: these are terms describing existence in the late twentieth century and many of the theories concerning that existence. Postmodernism captures the hollowing out and collapse of belief in human "progress" and other universal truths, ones often associated with the Enlightenment and "modern" era generally. Poststructuralism signals a similar failure of belief in human ability to manipulate and discover the truths underlying language, ideals which the linguistic movement known as "structuralism" often articulated or implicitly endorsed. Both are associated also with the recognition that such truths are socially constructed (see Social constructionism) and politically inflected (see Identity politics above).

Queer theory: this theoretical movement from the 1990s includes the work of Judith Butler, Diana Fuss, and others, who used Foucauldian and poststructuralist insights to challenge aggressively social definitions of the "normal" and "natural" in sexuality and sexual identity.

Social constructionism: as opposed to "essentialism" (see above), social constructionism emphasizes that there are no transhistorical truths and no "essential" underpinnings to differences in genders, races, sexual orientations, etc. Differences and the values that are attached to them are socially constructed in that they result from traditions, religious beliefs, and conventions, ones that reflect who has held social power and the ability to influence or determine social definitions.

Subjectivity: often used interchangeably with the term "identity," subjectivity more accurately denotes our social constructs and consciousness of identity. We commonly speak of identity as a flat, one-dimensional concept, but subjectivity is much broader and more multifaceted; it is social and personal being that exists in negotiation with broad cultural definitions and our own ideals. We may have numerous discrete identities, of race, class, gender, sexual orientation, etc., and a subjectivity that is comprised of all of those facets, as well as our own imperfect awareness of our selves.

Symbolic order: this is Jacques Lacan's concept that is roughly analogous to Foucault's term "discourse" (see above). The symbolic order consists of language, beliefs, ideologies, and all other means of cultural valuation and meaning making, which an infant encounters very early in life and through which she or he is acculturated and given a social identity and value system.

Unconscious: this is Sigmund Freud's repository of all of the fears, hopes, dreams, and anxieties that exist below the level of our conscious awareness. Psychoanalytic and cultural theory generally uses the concept of the unconscious to point out that we can never be fully aware of and empowered over our selves, and that much remains hidden within our psyches that we can never control and that has a profound influence on our actions, values, and subjectivity.

BIBLIOGRAPHY

Adams, Robert M. (1983) *The Land and Literature of England*, New York: Norton.

Althusser, Louis (1971) *Lenin and Philosophy and Other Essays*, New York: Monthly Review Press.

Andrew, Edward (1988) *Shylock's Rights: A Grammar of Lockian Claims*, Toronto: University of Toronto Press.

Anzaldúa, Gloria (1999) *Borderlands/La Frontera: The New Mestiza*, 2nd edition, San Francisco: Aunt Lute Books.

Augustine, Saint (1909) *The Confessions of St Augustine*, trans. Edward Pusey, in *The Harvard Classics*, vol. 7, ed. Charles Eliot, New York: Collier and Son.

Bambi (1942), Disney Studios.

Bauman, Zygmunt (1995) *Life in Fragments: Essays in Postmodern Morality*, Oxford: Blackwell.

Beauvoir, Simone de (1974) *The Second Sex*, trans. H. M. Parshley, New York: Vintage.

Behn, Aphra (2000) *Oroonoko, or The Royal Slave*, in *The Norton Anthology of English Literature, Volume 1*, 7th edition, ed. M. H. Abrams, New York: W. W. Norton.

Belsey, Catherine (1991) "Constructing the Subject, Deconstructing the Text," in *Feminisms: An Anthology of Literary Theory and Criticism*, eds. Robyn Warhol and Diane Price Herndl, New Brunswick, NJ: Rutgers University Press.

Bersani, Leo (1986) *The Freudian Body: Psychoanalysis and Art*, New York: Columbia University Press.

Bhabha, Homi K. (1994) *The Location of Culture*, London: Routledge.

Black, Jeremy (1996) *A History of the British Isles*, New York: St. Martins Press.

Bronte, Charlotte (1982) *Jane Eyre*, New York: Signet.

Brooks, Gwendolyn (1986) "Boy Breaking Glass," in *British and American Poets, Chaucer to the Present*, eds. W. Jackson Bate and David Perkins, p. 872, San Diego: Harcourt.

Browne, Alice (1987) *The Eighteenth Century Feminist Mind*, Detroit: Wayne State University Press.

Butler, Judith (1991) "Imitation and Gender Insubordination," in *Inside/Out: Lesbian Theory, Gay Theories*, ed. Diana Fuss, London: Routledge.

—— (1993) *Bodies that Matter: On the Discursive Limits of "Sex,"* London: Routledge.

—— (1997) *The Psychic Life of Power: Theories in Subjection*, Stanford: Stanford University Press.

—— (1999) *Gender Trouble: Feminism and the Subversion of Identity*, 10th anniversary edition, London: Routledge.

Camus, Albert (1972) *A Happy Death*, trans. Richard Howard, New York: Knopf.

Case, Sue-Ellen (1991) "Tracking the Vampire," *Differences* 3.2: 1-20.

Cassirer, Ernst (1951) *The Philosophy of the Enlightenment*, trans. Fritz Koelln and James Pettegrove, Boston: Beacon Press.

Childs, Peter (2000) *Modernism*, London: Routledge.

Chitty, Susan (1975) *The Beast and the Monk: A Life of Charles Kingsley*, New York: Mason/Charter.

Crosby, Christina (1992) "Dealing with Differences," in *Feminists Theorize the Political*, eds. Judith Butler and Joan W. Scott, London: Routledge.

Davies, Tony (1997) *Humanism*, London: Routledge.

Day, Gary (2001) *Class*, London: Routledge.

Deleuze, Gilles and Guattari, Feliz (1983) *Anti-Oedipus: Capitalism and Schizophrenia*, trans. Robert Hurley *et al.*, Minneapolis: University of Minnesota Press.

Deleuze, Gilles and Guattari, Felix (1987) *A Thousand Plateaus: Capitalism and Schizophrenia*, trans. Brian Massumi, Minneapolis: University of Minnesota Press.

Descartes, René (1968) *Discourse on Method and The Meditations*, trans. F. E. Sutcliffe, London: Penguin.

Douglass, Frederick (1973) *Narrative of the Life of Frederick Douglass*, Garden City, NY: Anchor Books.

Du Bois, W. E. B. (1989) *The Souls of Black Folks*, New York: Bantam.

Durkheim, Émile (1982) *The Rules of Sociological Method and Selected Texts on Sociology and Method*, trans. W. D. Halls, New York: The Free Press.

—— (1984) *The Division of Labor in Society*, trans. W. D. Halls, New York: The Free Press.

—— (1976) *Marxism and Literary Criticism*, Berkeley: University of California Press.

Eagleton, Terry (1991) *Ideology: An Introduction*, London: Verso.

Easthope, Antony (1999) *The Unconscious*, London: Routledge.

Edgar, Andrew and Sedgwick, Peter (eds.) (1999) *Key Concepts in Cultural Theory*, London: Routledge.

Eliot, George (1981a) *Middlemarch*, New York: Signet.

—— (1981b) *The Mill on the Floss*, New York: Signet.

—— (1992a) "Margaret Fuller and Mary Wollstonecraft," in *Selected Critical Writings*, by George Eliot, Oxford: Oxford University Press.

—— (1992b) "Silly Novels by Lady Novelists," in *Selected Critical Writings*, by George Eliot, Oxford: Oxford University Press.

—— (1995) *Daniel Deronda*, London: Penguin.

Eliot, T. S. (1962) "The Love Song of J. Alfred Prufrock," in *The Waste Land and Other Poems*, San Diego: Harcourt.

Falzon, Christopher (1998) *Foucault and Social Dialogue: Beyond Fragmentation*, London: Routledge.

Fanon, Frantz (1967) *Black Skin, White Masks*, trans. Charles Markmann, New York: Grove Press.

Foucault, Michel (1972) *The Archeology of Knowledge and The Discourse on Language*, trans. A. M. Sheridan Smith, New York: Pantheon Books.

—— (1990) *The History of Sexuality, Volume 1: An Introduction*, trans. Robert Hurley, New York: Vintage.

—— (1998) "Foucault," in *Aesthetics, Method, and Epistemology, Essential Works of Foucault, 1954–1984*, vol. 2, ed. James D. Faubion, trans. Robert Hurley *et al.*, New York: The New Press.

—— (2000) "The Subject and Power," in *Power, Essential Works of Foucault, 1954–1984*, vol. 3, ed. James D. Faubion, trans. Robert Hurley *et al.*, New York: The New Press.

Freud, Sigmund (1957a) "Beyond the Pleasure Principle," in *A General Selection From the Works of Sigmund Freud*, ed. John Rickman, Garden City, NY: Doubleday Anchor.

—— (1957b) "From 'An Autobiographical Study,'" in *A General Selection From the Works of Sigmund Freud*, ed. John Rickman, Garden City, NY: Doubleday Anchor.

—— (1957c) "A Note on the Unconscious in Psychoanalysis," in *A General Selection From the Works of Sigmund Freud*, ed. John Rickman, Garden City, NY: Doubleday Anchor.

Friedman, Lawrence M. (1999) *The Horizontal Society*, New Haven, CT: Yale University Press.

Frosh, Stephen (1999) *The Politics of Psychoanalysis: An Introduction to Freudian and Post-Freudian Theory*, New York: New York University Press.

Fuller, Margaret (1971) *Woman in the Nineteenth Century*, New York: Norton.

Fuss, Diana (1989) *Essentially Speaking: Feminism, Nature and Difference*, London: Routledge.

—— (ed.) (1991) *Inside/Out: Lesbian Theories, Gay Theories*, London: Routledge.

—— (1995) *Identification Papers*, London: Routledge.

Gabilondo, Joseba (1995) "Postcolonial Cyborgs: Subjectivity in the Age of Cybernetic Reproduction," in *The Cyborg Handbook*, ed. Chris Hables Gray, London: Routledge.

Gagnier, Regenia (1991) *Subjectivities: A History of Self-Representation in Britain, 1832–1920*, Oxford: Oxford University Press.

Garber, Linda (2001) *Identity Poetics: Race, Class, and the Lesbian-Feminist Roots of Queer Theory*, New York: Columbia University Press.

Gates, Henry Louis (1985a) "Editor's Introduction: Writing 'Race' and the Difference It Makes," in *"Race," Writing, and Difference*, ed. Henry Louis Gates, Chicago: University of Chicago Press.

—— (1985b) "Talking that Talk," in *"Race," Writing, and Difference*, ed. Henry Louis Gates, Chicago: University of Chicago Press.

Gay, John (1979) *The Beggar's Opera*, in *The Signet Classic Book of Eighteenth- and Nineteenth-Century British Drama*, ed. Katherine Rodgers, New York: Signet.

Giddens, Anthony (1990) *The Consequences of Modernity*, Stanford: Stanford University Press.

—— (1991) *Modernity and Self-Identity: Self and Society in the Late Modern Age*, Stanford: Stanford University Press.

—— (1992) *The Transformation of Intimacy: Sexuality, Love and Eroticism in Modern Societies*, Stanford: Stanford University Press.

Gilman, Charlotte Perkins (1995) *The Yellow Wall-Paper and Other Stories*, Oxford: Oxford University Press.

Glover, David and Kaplan, Cora (2000) *Genders*, London: Routledge.

Gower, John (1962) *The Major Latin Works of John Gower*, trans. Eric Stockton, Seattle: University of Washington Press.

Gray, Chris Hables (2001) *Cyborg Citizen: Politics in the Posthuman Age*, London: Routledge.

Greenblatt, Stephen (1980) *Renaissance Self-Fashioning: From More to Shakespeare*, Chicago: University of Chicago Press.

Hall, Donald E. (1994) "On the Making and Unmaking of Monsters: Christian Socialism, Muscular Christianity, and the Metaphorization of Class Conflict," in *Muscular Christianity: Embodying the Victorian Age*, ed. Donald E. Hall, Cambridge: Cambridge University Press.

—— (1996a) *Fixing Patriarchy: Feminism and Mid-Victorian Male Novelists*, New York: New York University Press.

—— (1996b) "Bambi on Top," *Children's Literature Association Quarterly*, 21.3: 120–25.

—— (2003) *Queer Theories*, Basingstoke: Palgrave Macmillan.

Halperin, David (1995) *Saint Foucault: Towards a Gay Hagiography*, Oxford: Oxford University Press.

Hamilton, Paul (1996) *Historicism*, London: Routledge.

Haraway, Donna J. (1991) *Simians, Cyborgs, and Women: The Reinvention of Nature*, New York: Routledge.

Hawkes, David (1996) *Ideology*, London: Routledge.

Hegel, G. W. F. (1977) *Phenomenology of Spirit*, trans. A. V. Miller, Oxford: Oxford University Press.

Henderson, Mae Gwendolyn (1994) "Speaking in Tongues: Dialogics, Dialectics and the Black Woman Writer's Literary Tradition," in *Colonial Discourse and Post-Colonial Theory: A Reader*, eds. Patrick Williams and Laura Chrisman, New York: Columbia University Press.

hooks, bell (1994) "Postmodern Blackness," in *Colonial Discourse and Post-Colonial Theory: A Reader*, eds. Patrick Williams and Laura Chrisman, New York: Columbia University Press.

Houghton, Walter (1957) *The Victorian Frame of Mind, 1830–1870*, New Haven, CT: Yale University Press.

Jacobs, Harriet (2000) *Incidents in the Life of a Slave Girl*, New York: Signet.

Jaspers, Karl (1962) *Kant*, trans. Ralph Manheim, New York: Harvest.

Jefferson, Thomas (1975) *The Portable Thomas Jefferson*, ed. Merrill D. Peterson, New York: Penguin.

Kant, Immanuel (2001) *Basic Writings of Kant*, ed. Allen W. Wood, New York: Modern Library.

Kavanagh, James (1995) "Ideology," in *Critical Terms for Literary Study*, 2nd edition, eds. Frank Lentricchia and Thomas McLaughlin, Chicago: University of Chicago Press.

Kincaid, Jamaica (1997) *My Brother*, New York: The Noonday Press.

Kingsley, Charles *et al.* (1848) *Politics for the People*, London.

Kirsch, Max (2000) *Queer Theory and Social Change*, London: Routledge.

Kristeva, Julia (1998) "The Subject in Process," trans. Patrick ffrench, in *The Tel Quel Reader*, eds. Patrick ffrench and Roland-Francois Lack, London: Routledge.

Lacan, Jacques (1977) *Ecrits: A Selection*, trans. Alan Sheridan, New York: Norton.

—— (1981) *The Seminar of Jacques Lacan Book XI: The Four Fundamental Concepts of Psychoanalysis*, trans. Alan Sheridan, New York: Norton.

—— (1991a) *The Seminar of Jacques Lacan Book I: Freud's Papers on Technique, 1953–1954*, trans. John Forrester, New York: Norton.

—— (1991b) *The Seminar of Jacques Lacan Book II: The Ego in Freud's Theory and in the Technique of Psychoanalysis, 1954–1955*, trans. Sylvana Tomaselli, New York: Norton.

—— (1997) *The Seminar of Jacques Lacan Book VII: The Ethics of Psychoanalysis, 1959–1960*, trans. Dennis Porter, New York: Norton.

Langer, Beryl (1991) "Emile Durkheim," in *A Guide to Central Thinkers: Social Theory*, ed. Peter Beilharz, Sydney: Allen & Unwin.

Lavine, T.Z (1984) *From Socrates to Sartre: The Philosophic Quest*, New York: Bantam Books.

Leahey, Thomas Hardy (1987) *A History of Psychology: Main Currents in Psychological Thought*, 2nd edition, Englewood Cliffs, NJ: Prentice-Hall.

Lee, Ang, dir. (1993) *The Wedding Banquet*.

Levy, Neil (2002) *Sartre*, Oxford: Oneworld Publications.

Locke, John (1975) *An Essay Concerning Human Understanding*, ed. Peter Nidditch, Oxford: Oxford University Press.

Loomba, Ania (1998) *Colonialism/Postcolonialism*, London: Routledge.

Lorde, Audre (1984) *Sister Outsider: Speeches and Essays*, Trumansburg, NY: The Crossing Press.

Lowe, E. J. (1995) *Locke on Human Understanding*, London: Routledge.

Luther, Martin (1910) "Concerning Christian Liberty," trans. R. S. Grignon, in *The Harvard Classics*, vol. 36, ed. Charles Eliot, New York: Collier and Son.

—— (1957) *On the Bondage of the Will*, trans J. I. Packer and O. R. Johnston, Westwood, NJ: Revell.

Machiavelli, Niccolò (1999) *The Prince*, trans. George Bull, London: Penguin.

Marks, Elaine (2001) "Some Final Words: An Interview with Elaine Marks," in *Professions: Conversations on the Future of Literary and Cultural Studies*, ed. Donald E. Hall, Urbana, IL: University of Illinois Press.

Marx, Karl (1970) *A Contribution to the Critique of Political Economy*, ed. Maurice Dobb, New York: International Publishers.

Marx, Karl and Engels, Friedrich (1978) "Manifesto of the Communist Party," in *The Marx–Engels Reader*, 2nd edition, ed. Robert C. Tucker, New York: Norton.

Massumi, Brian (1992) *A User's Guide to Capitalism and Schizophrenia: Deviations From Deleuze and Guattari*, Minneapolis: University of Minnesota Press.

Mestrovic, Stjepan (1998) *Anthony Giddens: The Last Modernist*, London: Routledge.

Mill, Harriet Taylor (1970) "Enfranchisement of Women," in *Essays on Sex Equality*, ed. Alice Rossi, Chicago: University of Chicago Press.

Mill, John Stuart (1975) "The Subjection of Women," in *Three Essays*, by John Stuart Mill, Oxford: Oxford University Press.

Moi, Toril (1985) *Sexual/Textual Politics*, London: Methuen.

Moran, Joe (2002) *Interdisciplinarity*, London: Routledge.

Murfin, Ross and Ray, Supryia (1997) *The Bedford Glossary of Critical and Literary Terms*, Boston: Bedford Books.

Nehamas, Alexander (1985) *Nietzsche: Life as Literature*, Cambridge, MA: Harvard University Press.

Nietzsche, Friedrich (1968) *The Will to Power*, trans. Walter Kaufmann and R. J. Hollingdale, New York: Vintage Books.

—— (1969) *On the Genealogy of Morals and Ecce Homo*, trans. Walter Kaufmann and R. J. Hollingdale, New York: Vintage Books.

—— (1974) *The Gay Science*, trans. Walter Kaufmann, New York: Vintage Books.

Plato (1973) *The Republic and Other Works*, trans. B. Jowett, Garden City, NY: Anchor Books.

Robbins, Ruth (2000) *Literary Feminisms*, Houndmills: Macmillan.

Roudinesco, Elisabeth (1997) *Jacques Lacan*, trans. Barbara Bray, New York: Columbia University Press.

Rubin, Gayle (1993) "Thinking Sex: Notes for a Radical Theory of the Politics of Sexuality," in *The Lesbian and Gay Studies Reader*, eds. Henry Abelove, Michele Aina Barale, and David Halperin, London: Routledge.

Sancho, Ignatius (2000) "Letter to Jack Wingrave," in *The Norton Anthology of English Literature, Volume 1*, 7th edition, ed. M. H. Abrams, New York: W. W. Norton.

Sartre, Jean-Paul (1975) "Existentialism is a Humanism," in *Existentialism from Dostoevsky to Sartre*, ed. Walter Kaufmann, New York: New American Library.

—— (1992) *Being and Nothingness*, trans. Hazel Barnes, New York: Washington Square Press.

Sawicki, Jana (1991) *Disciplining Foucault: Feminism, Power, and the Body*, London: Routledge.

Scott, Ridley, dir. (1982) *Blade Runner*, director's cut, 1991.

Searle, John (1994) *The Rediscovery of the Mind*, Cambridge, MA: The MIT Press.

Sedgwick, Eve (1993) *Tendencies*, Durham, NC: Duke University Press.

Shakespeare, William (1992) *Hamlet*, eds. Barbara Mowat and Paul Werstine, New York: Washington Square Press.

Singer, Peter (2001) *Hegel: A Very Short Introduction*, Oxford: Oxford University Press.

Skinner, Quentin (2000) *Machiavelli: A Very Short Introduction*, Oxford: Oxford University Press.

Smiles, Samuel (no date) *Self-Help*, Boston: Estes & Lauriat.

Sophocles (1967) "Antigone," in *The Complete Plays of Sophocles*, trans. Richard Jebb, pp. 115–47, New York: Bantam Books.

Spivak, Gayatri Chakravorty (1988) "Can the Subaltern Speak?" in *Marxism and the Interpretation of Culture*, eds. Cary Nelson and Lawrence Grossberg, Urbana, IL: University of Illinois Press.

Stavrakakis, Yannis (1991) *Lacan and the Political*, London: Routledge.

Sullivan, Roger (1994) *An Introduction to Kant's Ethics*, Cambridge: Cambridge University Press.

Swift, Jonathan (1998) *Gulliver's Travels*, ed. Paul Turner, Oxford: Oxford University Press.

Taylor, Charles (1975) *Hegel*, Cambridge: Cambridge University Press.

—— (1989) *Sources of the Self: The Making of the Modern Identity*, Cambridge, MA: Harvard University Press.

Thomson, Garrett (2000a) *On Descartes*, Belmont, CA: Wadsworth.

—— (2000b) *On Kant*, Belmont, CA: Wadsworth.

Thurschwell, Pamela (2000) *Sigmund Freud*, London: Routledge.

Tong, Rosemarie (1989) *Feminist Thought: A Comprehensive Introduction*, Boulder, CO: Westview Press.

Warner, Michael (1993) "Introduction," in *Fear of a Queer Planet: Queer Politics and Social Theory*, ed. Michael Warner, Minneapolis: University of Minnesota Press.

Weedon, Chris (1987) *Feminist Practice and Poststructuralist Theory*, Oxford: Basil Blackwell.

Wollstonecraft, Mary (1988) *A Vindication of the Rights of Woman*, Norton Critical Edition, ed. Carol Poston, New York: Norton.

Woolf, Virginia (1956) *Orlando*, San Diego: Harcourt.

—— (1981) *Mrs. Dalloway*, San Diego: Harcourt.

Zizek, Slavoj (1999) *The Ticklish Subject: The Absent Centre of Political Ontology*, London: Verso.

INDEX

Adams, Robert M. 11
agency 5–8, 10, 14, 15, 21, 27, 29,
    41, 42, 44, 46, 48, 52, 62–66,
    68, 70, 71, 74, 77, 80–82, 87,
    88, 90, 95, 97, 99, 101, 102, 10,
    105, 107, 109, 110, 111, 113–16,
    118–30
Althusser, Louis 33, 84–90, 91, 97,
    99
Anzaldúa, Gloria 112–14
Arendt, Hannah 29
Aristotle 8

Bauman, Zygmunt 129
Beauvoir, Simone de 98–99
Behn, Afra 34–35
Belsey, Catherine 99–100, 108
Benhabib, Seyla 29
Bersani, Leo 102
Bhabha, Homi 114–15
Black, Jeremy 11
Black Death 11
Bosch, Hieronymus 83
Brecht, Bertolt 30
Bronte, Charlotte 46
Brooks, Gwendolyn 96–97
Browne, Alice 39
Butler, Judith 63, 88, 94–95, 104–06,
    125–28

Camus, Albert 67, 68, 74–77
Case, Sue-Ellen 106
Cassirer, Ernst 14
Chartism 56–57
Chaucer, Geoffrey 13
Childs, Peter 63, 64, 68
Cixous, Hélène 101

class 10–11, 14, 30–32, 38, 46, 49,
    50–57, 62, 64, 66, 84–90, 97, 112,
    116, 128, 129
cogito 3, 19–20, 82, 123, 130
Comte, Auguste 59
Conrad, Joseph 74
Copernicus 17
Crosby, Christina 122
cyborgs 120–24

Dali, Salvador 84
Darwin, Charles 4, 59, 68, 69
Davies, Tony 18, 87, 91
Day, Gary 10, 50, 55
Deleuze, Gilles 102, 107, 119–20
Descartes, René 3, 16, 19–23, 27, 60, 82,
    120, 123, 130
Disney 89–90
Douglass, Frederick 36–37
Du Bois, W. E. B. 38–39, 110
Duke of Montague 35
Durkheim, Émile 58–59

Eagleton, Terry 82, 88, 90
Easthope, Anthony 61
Edgar, Andrew 18, 23–24
Eliot, George 46–49
Eliot, T. S. 63–64
Emerson, Ralph Waldo 66
Engels, Friedrich 51–54
Enlightenment 23–24, 32, 39, 45,
    91
epistemology 4
Equiano, Olaudah 36
ethics 8–9, 20, 22, 27–28, 30, 38,
    72–74
existentialism 23, 67–77

Falzon, Christopher 91, 95
Fanon, Frantz 114–15
feminism 39–49, 97–102, 103, 110
Foucault, Michel 33, 40, 90–97, 102–03, 109, 110, 115
French Revolution 32, 50
Freud, Sigmund 59–67, 76, 78–79, 91, 97, 99, 102
Friedman, Lawrence M. 1–2, 125
Frosch, Stephen 62–64
Fuller, Margaret 43, 45–47, 66
Fuss, Diana 101–02

Gabilondo, Joseba 122–23
Gagnier, Regenia 2–3
Galileo 17
Garber, Linda 111
Gates, Henry Louis 34
Gay, John 30–31, 37
gender 1, 2, 13–14, 28, 32, 39–49, 62, 65, 66, 88–90, 95–110, 112, 116, 117, 126–28
Genet, Jean 74
George III 36
Giddens, Anthony 126, 128
Gide, André 74
Gilman, Charlotte Perkins 64–65
Glover, David 40, 127
Gower, John 12
Gramsci, Antonio 87
Gray, Chris 122
Greenblatt, Stephen 6
Grimm Brothers 89
Guattari, Felix 102, 107, 119–120

Halperin, David 91
Hamilton, Paul 16
Haraway, Donna 120–22, 124
Havel, Vaclav 30
Hegel, G. W. F. 50–52, 55, 56
Henderson, Mae Gwendolyn 112
homosexuality 93, 102–11, 113, 116
hooks, bell 110–12, 114

Houghton, Walter 66
Hume, David 27, 34

Inquisition 14

Jacobs, Harriet 37
James II 26
Jaspers, Karl 28
Joan of Arc 13–14

Kant, Immanuel 27–29, 31, 32, 34, 37, 55, 73
Kaplan, Cora 40, 127
Kavanagh, James 84, 88
Kierkegaard, Søren 68
Kincaid, Jamaica 116–17
Kingsley, Charles 56–57
Kirsch, Max 90
Kristeva, Julia 99–101

Lacan, Jacques 33, 63, 78–84, 87, 97, 99, 100
Langer, Beryl 58–59
Langland, William 11
Lavine, T. Z. 7, 20
Leahey, Thomas 59
Lee, Ang 107–09
Levy, Neil 67
Locke, John 24–27, 33–35, 37, 39, 42, 45
Loomba, Ania 114, 115
Lorde, Audre 110–11, 114
Lowe, E. J. 25
Luther, Martin 14–15, 18

Machiavelli, Niccolo 18–19, 22
Marks, Elaine 4
Marx, Karl 50–57, 85, 87, 91
Massumi, Brian 120
Mestrovic, Stjepan 126
Mill, Harriet Taylor 43–45, 49
Mill, John Stuart 43–45, 49, 50, 51
Moi, Toril 98, 100
Moran, Joe 4
Murfin, Ross 4

Nehamas, Alexander 69, 72
New Historicism 16
Nietzsche, Friedrich 19, 67–76

objectivity 3, 24, 27–28, 31, 57, 59, 60
ontology 4
overdetermination 17

Peasant's Revolt 11–12
Perrault, Charles 89
Plato 7–10
postcoloniality 36, 116–17, 122–23, 128
Prince, Mary 36
psychology 2, 44, 48, 57–67

queer theory 103–09

race and ethnicity 1, 2, 32–39, 59, 62, 66, 90, 107–17, 126–128
Ray, Supryia 4
Robbins, Ruth 42, 50
Roudinesco, Elizabeth 79, 82
Rousseau, Jean-Jacques 39–41
Rubin, Gayle 103

Saint Augustine 9–10, 15
Saint Francis 7
Sancho, Ignatius 35–36
Sartre, Jean-Paul 67, 68, 71–74, 76, 98
satire 29–30
Saussure, Ferdinand 91
Sawicki, Jana 90–91
Scott, Ridley 123–24
Searle, John 118–19
Sedgwick, Eve 107
Sedgwick, Peter 18, 23–24
self-help 1, 22–23, 47, 49, 66–67, 71

sexuality 2, 28, 60, 64, 92, 93, 97–109, 112, 116, 117, 127, 128
Shakespeare, William 21–23
Singer, Peter 51, 52
Skinner, Quentin 19
slavery 32–39
Smiles, Samuel 66–67
social construction 2, 35, 40–42, 47, 90, 92, 96, 98, 100–01, 105
sociology 2, 58, 59
Socrates 7–8
Sophocles 8–9, 12, 21–22
Spencer, Herbert 59, 68
Spivak, Gayatri 113–14
Stavrakakis, Yannis 82–84
subjectivity (defined) 2–4, 15, 25
Sullivan, Roger 28
Swift, Jonathan 29

Taylor, Charles 6–7, 9–10, 15, 17, 20–21, 24–26, 33, 54, 55, 60
Thomson, Garrett 20, 27
Thoreau, Henry David 66
Thurschwell, Pamela 60–61
Tong, Rosemarie 42

Warner, Michael 104
Weedon, Chris 100–101
Wells, H. G. 123
William III 26
Wingrave, Jack 35
Wollstonecraft, Mary 40–43, 45–47
Woolf, Virginia 64–65, 73, 95–96
Wundt, Wilhelm 59

Yeats, William Butler 73–74

Zizek, Slavoj 83

eBooks – at www.eBookstore.tandf.co.uk

A library at your fingertips!

eBooks are electronic versions of printed books. You can
store them on your PC/laptop or browse them online.

They have advantages for anyone needing rapid access
to a wide variety of published, copyright information.

eBooks can help your research by enabling you to
bookmark chapters, annotate text and use instant searches
to find specific words or phrases. Several eBook files would
fit on even a small laptop or PDA.

NEW: Save money by eSubscribing: cheap, online access
to any eBook for as long as you need it.

Annual subscription packages

We now offer special low-cost bulk subscriptions to
packages of eBooks in certain subject areas. These are
available to libraries or to individuals.

For more information please contact
webmaster.ebooks@tandf.co.uk

We're continually developing the eBook concept, so
keep up to date by visiting the website.

www.eBookstore.tandf.co.uk